Classroom Research

for Teachers:

A Practical Guide

Classroom Research

for Teachers:

A Practical Guide

Rita A. Moore

Associate Professor of Education,
University of Montana–Western

Christopher-Gordon Publishers, Inc.
Norwood, Massachusetts

Credits

Every effort has been made to contact copyright holders for permission to reproduce borrowed material where necessary. We apologize for any oversights and would be happy to rectify them in future printings.

Excerpt from *Powerful Writing* by Marcia Treat. Copyright © 2001 by Curriculum Solutions, Inc. Reprinted by permission.

Material adapted from Wollman-Bonilla, J. *Family message journals: Teaching writing through family involvement.* Copyright © 2002 by the National Council of teachers of English. Reprinted by permission.

Sample action research projects conducted by teachers enrolled in a graduate course at Washburn University, Kansas. Used by permission of students.

Student work used by permission.

Christopher-Gordon Publishers, Inc.
1502 Providence Highway, Suite #12
Norwood, Massachusetts 02062
800-934-8322
781-762-5577

Printed in the United States of America

10 9 8 7 6 5 4 3 2   09 08 07 06 05

ISBN: 1-929024-65-7
Library of Congress Catalogue Number: 2003109066

Table of Contents

Dedication

I would like to dedicate this book to the teachers of Pleasant Hill, Rochester, Elmont, Lyman, and Shawnee Heights Elementary Schools in Topeka, Kansas, who, through their continued classroom research and practice, endeavor to enrich the teaching and learning communities in which they work. And, a special thanks to teachers from other schools, like Karen, Marilee, Lisa, and Kelli, whose work in classroom research sets a standard for us all.

Preface

This book was written for elementary and middle school classroom teachers, as well as for preservice teachers and student teachers who wish to further understand and appreciate the role of teacher as researcher. In this writing, you will meet both veteran and novice teachers who strengthened their teaching, and subsequently, student learning, through classroom research.

Many of the teachers introduced are mentor teachers to preservice and student teachers in a Professional Development School (PDS) partnership called *Teaching and Learning Communities*. During the early development of the PDS, 28 teachers enrolled in a one-credit graduate course focused on using action research in the classroom setting. This prompted several teachers to conduct their research in collaboration with the teaching intern they supervised or to utilize one another as peer reviewers for their separate projects.

In thinking about a common thread that introduces these professional colleagues and friends, I realize that they all expressed interest in utilizing classroom research methodology for professional development and student learning. Their stories, advice, and examples indeed demonstrate that classroom research provides a rich resource for achieving greater student learning success, as well as contributing to the image of the teacher as a confident and well-informed professional.

I believe that administrators and curriculum directors will gain valuable insight from the voices of these teachers, particularly if they are in the process of providing frameworks for classroom research in their schools and districts. This book is about authentic research to inform, refresh, and guide instructional practice at many levels. As a teacher and teacher educator of over 25 years, I feel that the examples and vignettes in this book will also provide university professors with a text that draws heavily from the actual experiences of classroom teachers engaged in the process of learning from and about classroom action research.

Introduction

Do you ever wish you could clearly describe the effectiveness of your teaching decisions and actions on student learning? When was the last time you felt confident in making a very difficult instructional decision? Classroom research conducted by teachers is about finding systematic ways of examining patterns of learner response to inform our teaching actions and decisions. These patterns are the invaluable "nuggets of gold" that, when panned and sorted, will guide our daily teaching lives. This is a book with anecdotes and advice from practicing classroom teachers who, with action research, discovered a practical, effective means of continually monitoring and improving teaching and learning. Many of these teachers shared their findings with colleagues and administrators within their schools and school districts which, in turn, helped shape curriculum, as well as adding to the professional development of others.

Classroom research by teachers is a process not only for exploring teaching and learning outcomes but for valuing our teaching actions and beliefs (Cochran-Smith & Lytle, 1992). As a process, teacher research holds the potential to "radically alter" teaching and learning (Cochran-Smith & Lytle, 1993, p. 85). This suggests that through classroom research, teachers have the opportunity not only to inform day to day instructional decision making but to examine the beliefs behind their teaching actions, thus making explicit what might ordinarily be tacit in their understanding of teaching and learning.

It is important to remember that not all teachers have the same belief systems or instructional agendas, but we all learn from one another nevertheless. You will meet teachers in this book from multiple philosophical orientations and instructional styles. Classroom research establishes a forum for sharing and learning about many things common to classroom and school culture. No project is without value when conducted in the democratic spirit of classroom action research—examining our actions and the many voices of response from learners.

There are many uncharted patterns of teaching and learning present in our classrooms that provide important evidence for instructional decision making. However, unless these patterns are identified and used to inform instruction, teachers are left to rely on traditional trial and error methodology, leaving us vulnerable to public and professional criticism. This can be avoided if we demonstrate our use of classroom research as a reliable means of determining which instructional practices best support learner success. The growing acceptance of classroom research and its results have empowered us as teachers and leaders in our fields of educational expertise (McFarland & Stansell, 1993) to "make sense" of our teaching actions by examining and characterizing the pedagogical beliefs behind them.

Watson (1996) offers a rationale for including the study of teaching beliefs in classroom research: "Beliefs keep us sane. On Monday morning we don't have to reconstruct what it is we trust, what we know is credible, what we accept as true. We *are* our beliefs" (p. 213). Teachers can bring their own belief system into existence by examining evidence of the practice of those beliefs in their daily teaching (Watson, 1996), but the question of where the everyday classroom teacher finds such evidence often creates a dilemma. With a plan of action for gathering and analyzing evidence, the dilemma can be solved.

Classroom research conducted by teachers provides us with valuable firsthand insight into topics such as management, assessment practices, student perceptions of learning, effective teaching strategies, the influence of background on learning, and student learning preferences. It yields data that suggest opportunities for teachers, students, and parents to connect in meaningful, focused conversations about practical, daily evidence of student success and progress. It offers teachers opportunities to regularly validate what they know about their students' learning as well as their own teaching.

Current national teacher preparation standards developed by the National Council for Accreditation of Teacher Education (NCATE) and the Interstate New Teacher Assessment and Support Consortium (INTASC) ask that teachers understand the concept of classroom research—action research in particular—as a means for reflectively examining learner success through multiple lenses. There is, however, little emphasis on changing the way the teaching culture understands classroom research by teachers as an interpretive *tool* for documenting and improving teaching and learning (Darling-Hammond, 1997). Unless we as teachers experience the utility and accessibility of classroom research, we may never fully know the satisfaction of confident instructional decision making based on evidence from student work.

Teaching is re-searching (Brause & Mayher, 1991). It would be difficult to argue that good teaching does not involve investigating the impact of classroom instruction on student learning. The K–6 teachers in this book have discovered that incorporating simple action research strategies into teaching routines is fundamental to interpreting learner success. Teachers and administrators readily acknowledge that no longer can the teacher arbitrarily assign a grade or rubric value to student work. Parents and students want, and deserve to know how learning was determined, what that determination means for the student, and specific ways in which the curriculum supports or develops learner progress.

Demystifying Classroom Research

Classroom research need not be mysterious or impractical. It does not have to be experimental research conducted by strangers who may have never taught school, and it can be used to improve teaching and learning by the most novice teacher. It is also accessible; our classrooms are living documentaries of how learning takes place and why. When such evidence is ignored or dismissed in lieu of grades and percentages, teachers are disconnected from learners and disenfranchised as professional decision makers. Teaching becomes a function separate from learning.

The teachers whose reflections and examples from their classroom research are included in this book have in common the desire to improve their teaching and make better instructional choices. As well, they want to help others understand the value of classroom research. These teachers believe their classrooms can produce valuable evidence, "nuggets of gold," to support the strong element of change that is everpresent in daily pedagogical decision making. Their individual and collective experiences will highlight the multidimensional aspects of classroom research while demonstrating the utility of their research outcomes as guidelines for instructional decisions. Their voices and research outcomes were supported by five principals who valued and honored the teachers' efforts toward better understanding the learning needs of the students in their classrooms.

In chapter 1, you will meet two first-grade teachers who systematically and daily utilize student learning outcomes to inform their teaching. Throughout the text, you will hear from various teachers who utilize action research methodology to carry out classroom research in elementary and middle school classrooms. At the end of each chapter are a few of the questions which sprang from the ongoing discussion among teachers when they explored classroom research as an empowering dimension of teaching and learning. They are intended to be *conversation start-ers* for your own collegial discussions about classroom research.

As you read, please remember that the process of classroom research belongs to *you* as a teacher and learner. How you proceed has unlimited possibilities and, as all the teachers in this book have reiterated, no matter how simple or complex your project, you will discover patterns of teaching and learning of which you were previously unaware. You will find that classroom research is not intended to be an additional task; rather, a strategy for examining what you already do through a different perspective as you explore and document patterns of teaching and learning. I believe you will also recognize the utility of classroom research for communicating the relationship between responsible teaching and successful student learning with administrators, parents, and community.

Chapter 1

The Relationship Between Classroom Research and Teaching

any teachers have discovered the reflective and reflexive relationship between research and teaching. In discussing action research with teachers who implement this process into daily teaching, it is common to hear them say that they previously had no organized, informative way of monitoring their teaching actions. They may have depended largely on test scores or what they *thought* they were observing in the classroom. Of course, they used various formal and informal assessments, which were often linked to grades or meeting performance standards within a specific time frame. However, the "aha" moment for teachers who incorporated research into their daily teaching arrived when they were able to pinpoint patterns of learner response they never before realized.

One teacher compared classroom research to looking through a kaleidoscope. We observe different patterns depending on how the pieces are arranged as you turn the scope. What often happens in the research analysis process is the information that you may or may not have collected before reveals patterns of learner response quite different from what you expected, *or* had previously concluded. Reflecting on the patterns and making instructional changes based on authentic evidence (assignments, performance, observations of student work) is a natural part of this process for teachers who are experienced teacher researchers.

Meet Darlene and Cindy

Two colleagues, Darlene and Cindy, are first-grade teachers in a large rural school district. They are also practicing classroom researchers. On any given day during the language arts lesson, Darlene and Cindy may be observed taking running records of children reading orally, writing quick notes on student behaviors, finding time to listen to and document a retelling of a story, collecting writing samples for student portfolios, and later, looking for patterns of learner response in all of these data sources. As individual classroom teachers, they coordinate their research with their teaching. For example, they organize their time to make sure that over the span of six weeks they have taken running records (Clay, 1993; Clay, 2000) and completed a retelling over every student in their class. They each have a three-ring binder in which they collect and organize the data, divided by student names, then examine the oral readings from the students for patterns of phonological awareness, comprehension, and use of syntax.

As Cindy said, they might learn that a child is having difficulty with medial *"th"* phonemes in specific words or applying word-solving strategies (Pinnell & Fountas, 1998). They might also find that another child's accuracy in retelling has increased, leading them to determine what sorts of instruction has affected this progress. A quick look at lesson plans or their own teaching notes helps them to make this important pedagogical connection.

Taking running records is not the only form of student response these teachers systematically examine. Cindy and Darlene document the children's emergent spelling patterns by randomly collecting and analyzing samples of student work within time frames corresponding to the required progress reports of their district. They share their findings during informal meetings, at lunch, during recess duty, or as they prepare for parent/teacher conferences. This is classroom research—all documented, all discovered through patterns of learner response.

Darlene and Cindy have worked this simple research process into their daily teaching routines by choosing time frames and measurements of student outcomes from daily assignments and observations. Cindy explains just a few of the rewards that classroom research has given her: "I can now *show* parents what it means to say that spelling is emerging. They can *see* selected, ongoing samples of how their child is moving closer to conventional spellings or the use of writing conventions. If they can recognize the different ways spelling progress was facilitated, then they can also understand how they might parallel this process at home." And, Darlene reiterates, "It's simple, but it is truly meaningful to teaching and learning."

While much has been written about teacher research, the actual preparation of teachers in the use of classroom research tools is limited. Not every teacher is as experienced and confident as Cindy and Darlene in using classroom data to inform instruction; therefore, in this book I will introduce some tools and methods commonly associated with action research in helping you get started. Action research methodology, as presented here, is designed to help you become better skilled in formulating questions about your teaching. As you continue to read, you will recognize the rich data sources of the classroom, construct methods for gathering and analyzing the data, and find appropriate, meaningful ways for sharing the implications of your findings with principals, colleagues, students, and parents.

As a teacher educator and teacher researcher, I have found it best to start out with a plan that is fairly straightforward. Although you might not follow this process explicitly, there is benefit in understanding the various steps in the action research process explained in the chapters that follow. Stories and advice from the teachers who used this process to introduce the element of research into their classrooms will guide you.

Chapter Summary

This chapter is an introduction to the relationship between teaching and researching. I encourage you to think about your own classroom as a rich, scarcely tapped source of information on teaching and learning. Consider the children whose learning outcomes puzzle you, or think about a particular teaching approach or method you would like to implement and how you will know when that approach or method is successful.

Teaching and researching are reciprocal processes. Defining ourselves as professionals capable of monitoring our own teaching and learning by making classroom research a daily part of our teaching lives demonstrates to us, our students, the community, and the administration that we are knowing, caring professionals whose experiences as researchers are integral to curriculum development and student learning success.

Conversation Starters . . .

- In what ways do you currently examine your own teaching and student learning with the purpose of informing instructional decision making?

- When have you ever wished you had more evidence on which to base a student's score or grade? Or, when have you ever wanted more information on how a teacher decided on a grade or a score for you?

- Explore the term "patterns of student learning." What are some patterns you have noticed in your own learning?

Chapter 2

Action Research:
Tools and Strategies
for Classroom Research

"Sing. Umty-tiddly, umty-too. Here we go gathering Nuts and May. Enjoy yourself. 'I am,' said Pooh. 'Some can,' said Eyore."

(A. A. Milne, 1926)

This chapter introduces and provides background for a simple classroom research model known as action research. It is my intent to demystify the traditional connotations of "research" and suggest you think of it as a state of mind (Hubbard & Power, 1999) closely akin to the concept of curiosity (Arhar, Holly, & Kasten, 2001). I invite you to view simple action research as an easily learned, adaptable, and manageable *process* of information gathering and synthesis that includes helpful steps and tools. The kind of information you gather and how you choose to use it is entirely up to your teaching and learning goals. It *can* be an enjoyable and rewarding experience.

History and Purpose of Action Research

Use of action research in education is not new. It emerged as a methodology for classroom research in the early 1940s with the work of psychologist Kurt Lewin, who urged researchers and practitioners to collaboratively address classroom issues and problems (Patterson, Santa, Short, & Smith, 1993). Lewin proposed that teachers investigate the personal and interpersonal communication gaps that kept them from understanding their own biases (Arhar, Holly, & Kasten, 2001; Lewin, 1946). In the early 1950s, with the work of Stephen Corey (1952; 1953), action research grew increasingly popular because of its direct association with reflective teaching (Schon, 1983; 1987). With the emergence of the work of John Elliot and Lawrence Stenhouse in the 1970s, action research gained an established place in education and classroom research methods. Elliot and Stenhouse formed the Collaborative Action Research Network (CARN), which encouraged action research with a qualitative orientation. This included both experimental and naturalistic methods, in which the "context, questions, purposes, and participants drive the appropriateness of methods" (Arhar, Holly, & Kasten, 2001, p. 50).

Today, action research is defined within the realm of reflective teaching (Arhar, Holly, & Kasten, 2001; Cochran-Smith, & Lytle, 1993; Hubbard & Power, 1993; 1999; Schon, 1983). It is rapidly becoming a recognized source of professional development for teachers, particularly in teacher support groups, where the results of classroom research are shared (Lefever-Davis, 2002; National Commission on Teaching, 1996; Calhoun, 2002).

Action research presents a simple, reliable research process that may be used to focus teaching questions, and gather, organize, and interpret the many classroom data sources which reflect student responses to teaching. It provides basic tools and strategies, leading to a more comprehensive way of thinking about classroom research. Once familiar with the components of the action research process, you can broaden and modify it to fit individual classroom research needs and goals. As a teacher, you will begin to conceptualize classroom research as an ongoing assessment process in which you continually implement the tools and strategies of action research to view daily teaching and learning. In fact, you are probably already following some of the steps as a part of your daily teaching routine, but the process completed as a whole is very powerful and empowering.

Meet Barbara and Debbie

Barbara, a kindergarten teacher of 25 years, describes her first experience with classroom action research: "We do all these things almost daily as teachers, but I just never knew how to organize what I was observing in such a way that it systematically informed my teaching." Barbara studied how changing one aspect of a literacy program she had been using for several years affected the retention of letters and letter sounds of her kindergarten students, as well as their motivation to learn them.

Debbie, a fifth-grade teacher of over 15 years, also had just finished her first attempt at classroom research. She adds:

Classroom research made my teaching more meaningful. For example, I discovered how powerful it is to have student input when designing performance rubrics. Prior to my project, I designed the rubrics, but I learned that with student input came greater ownership and increased motivation and performance. They expected as much of themselves as I did . . . sometimes more!

These two experienced teachers were new to action research as a classroom research and assessment process; however, in six short weeks, both were so pleased with what they discovered that they made plans to expand their projects into the next year.

After many years of teaching, as well as working with other classroom teachers, I advocate the use of this easy and effective model as a template for exploring patterns of learner response and guiding instructional practice. To broaden my own professional development and awareness of learning patterns, I have conducted classroom research in my language arts classroom—at the middle school and university level. As various steps are explained in the rest of the book, I will include comments and stories from teachers who were in various stages of acquiring classroom research skills. While many of the projects are literacy related, I have included studies in math, social studies, and classroom behavior management as well. And, although the examples spring from the experiences of elementary and middle school teachers, the process of classroom action research may be adapted to any grade-level setting.

Following are basic steps in conducting action research for beginning researchers. They are explained utilizing more in-depth experiences from teachers in subsequent chapters, but for now, you can see the "big picture" with a few brief examples. It is important to remember that this is an organic process that may require some adjustment, depending on individual teaching classrooms and school settings. For example, you may discover that you need to change one of your data sources or rework one of your research questions as a result of a modification of schedule, or perhaps some newly identified learning needs of your students. You may discover, as did several of the teachers in this book, that it is helpful to modify the wording of a research question to better capture your data. It is also likely that one or more of your data sources more adequately addresses a question than the one you originally intended. This is a fluid, flexible process—much like teaching. And, since you are probably interested in conducting classroom research to inform your teaching, the results of your study *must* be useful to you.

How you choose to design your study largely depends on your research focus, your research questions, your personal teaching preferences, the available classroom data sources, how the data-gathering procedure fits into your daily classroom schedule, and how you decide to later analyze your findings. It is also important to realize that data you gather may be anecdotal (descriptive), quantitative (numerical measures), or a mixture of both. By way of example, you may choose to report your findings as numerically charted information on student learning or by noting strong patterns of student response that continually emerge in your teaching journal, anecdotal records, or notes to yourself at the end of the day.

Start with a very simple project and later expand. It is important to begin with an aspect of teaching and learning that really puzzles or interests you so that you will be truly engaged in the process. Approach your research by saying the phrase, "I wonder . . ." and brainstorm a quick list of things you have thought about changing or doing differently in your classroom. Perhaps there's a teaching strategy you have wanted to try or a management problem you cannot seem to solve. You may conduct whole-class, small-group, or single-case study projects. Remember, this is your research, your learning. Your research focus, time frame, and procedure are driven by you and by the normal routine of your classroom.

Classroom action research is "focused upon life and practices within classrooms and schools" (Arhar, Holly, & Kasten, 2001, p. 47).

Basic Steps in Conducting Classroom Action Research

1. Develop a research focus. Begin by identifying a learning situation that is particularly puzzling to you. It might be something that you have been wondering about adapting or adopting to change student learning, or it might be a hunch you have about students' responses to a particular program, management strategy, or teacher behavior.

2. Explore a little background related to your research focus. Read a journal article or two, consult the World Wide Web, or simply discuss the subject with a knowledgeable professional.

3. Decide which students (all class, a small group, a single case) will be participants in your classroom research. Unless you plan to publish or share your research at a conference, you do not need to have parental permission; however, it's always a good idea to inform your principal of your plans.

4. Write two or three open-ended questions about the problem or situation. For example: "How do graphic organizers influence students' use of details in creative writing?" Avoid broad, complicated questions like, "What is the correlation between standardized assessment and teacher-made tests?" Leave questions like these for people conducting formal research under controlled conditions that may be generalized across many classroom contexts. The questions you will write are focused, practical, and designed to provide information applicable primarily to your classroom.

5. Reexamine your research questions and determine where you can find evidence to address them. It is advisable to have at least two data sources for each question, and three if you plan to publish or present your work formally. Determine what you might use for baseline data, sometimes called "pre" and "post" assessment information.

6. Determine the time frame and procedure you will use to collect data; then collect your baseline of information. For example, your first set of data responses may serve as your baseline.

7. Continue to collect data over a three- to six-week period of time. You may wish to use a simple color-coding technique (explained more fully later) to keep the data organized.

8. At the end of your designated time frame, reread your coded data and see if you still agree with your markings. Change them as needed.

9. Reread all the sections coded to each one of the questions. Now, look for patterns in the responses you have coded to the questions and decide on categories or themes that emerge within the patterns. Categories or themes are subheadings which help you summarize, explain, and conceptualize learner responses.

10. Discuss your coding and patterns of response with a colleague to see if you have missed something. *Always* protect the anonymity of the students when discussing scores or other personal data.

11. Look at the data responses, and again, note the patterns you have identified and the categories that help organize the learner responses. Now, beneath each one, list their implications to you for teaching and learning.

12. Share this information with peers and colleagues in a setting that honors the importance of the research process as well as the findings.

Action Research: A Method for Conducting Classroom Research

Action research provides a springboard into broader extensions of everyday classroom research. Experienced classroom teachers, like Darlene and Cindy, daily utilize the components of action research such as data collection and analysis within the entire context of teaching, learning, and assessment. Instead of one action research project, they have multiple projects operating to yield many sources of information for their teaching. Research is a part of their instructional framework. For example, Darlene and Cindy monitor reading comprehension through retellings. Retellings are conducted as informal postreading activities in which the child "retells" all that he or she remembers after reading the selection orally, which is then discussed, commented upon, or embellished (Harp, 2000). These teachers have a system for conducting regular retellings, a way of collecting the information, and a time frame in which to analyze the information. Their research questions focus on the effectiveness of regular retellings to support reading comprehension, since retellings are not typically administered with running records (Clay, 2000). Darlene and Cindy report the results to parents and children by charting the patterns of progress evident in looking at each child's retelling scores. These records and scores are stored in the large, three-ring data binder maintained as part of the classroom assessment records.

Instead of focusing on the entire class, a teacher new to classroom research might decide to conduct a focused research inquiry with a particularly puzzling student, still using daily assignments and routine observations as data. For example, Cindy was having difficulty keeping a bipolar child focused on his writing. She noticed that he always physically shielded his writing in some way. On a hunch, she found a brightly colored cardboard learning carrel and asked him if he would like to work in the second-grade classroom in the carrel. Working in a classroom of "older" students was not degrading, and the second-grade teacher was willing to help monitor his progress. Cindy documented gains in the child's on-task writing within just a few weeks.

The process of classroom action research should be fluid. The key is learning how to put the parts together to make them useful to classroom teaching and learning. Critical to your success as a classroom researcher is the ability to be a good kid watcher (Goodman, 1978, 1996; Watson, 1996). Data gathering occurs as you are carefully watching and listening to children while they read, write, draw, and talk about their learning. Analysis is sorting and scrutinizing the data for recurring patterns that will help you decide if current classroom routines are working for the child or children you studied.

Other Uses for Classroom Research

More formal classroom research, such as that used to study curriculum or school culture, typically focuses on one or two research questions and analysis of data for outcomes that lead to more broad-based instructional decision making (Calhoun, 2002; Glanz, 1998). Classroom research may be used to assess the effectiveness of a particular teaching strategy over a short period of time by a group of teachers, or it may address a much more complex curricular change. For example, teachers interested in classroom management strategies may try a particular management plan to investigate its effects on the behaviors of a few or all of the students. Or, an entire school that chooses to adopt a curricular focus, such as the use of graphic organizers across the curriculum, may design, in tandem, an action research plan for investigating the effectiveness of graphic organizers on one or two student learning goals over a year's time.

In any case, the action research model provides classroom researchers with a format and method that will yield learner response patterns through a systematic data collection and analysis process. Once mastered, that format can be incorporated into daily classroom routines and used to substantiate learning outcomes in ways in which children, parents, and other teachers can participate. It may also be applied to larger, schoolwide studies.

Classroom research that follows the format of action research strengthens teaching and learning through informed choices. In classroom research where action research methodology is utilized, reflexivity becomes a part of the daily lives of teachers as they examine, then reflect on, their actions and whether or not those actions should be subject to change. Action research provides a problem-solving approach to the investigation of our teaching lives. There are many things that puzzle us as classroom teachers, but how many times do we actually formulate questions to focus our observations? When do we examine the rich data patterns from daily classroom assignments and learner interactions (teachers included) to reflect upon and view student responses to our teaching?

Action research inquiry projects may be formally conducted as graduate and undergraduate course requirements—usually as required projects in which the rudiments of ethnographic research are taught within the context of teacher training. The instructional decision making linked to teacher training in classroom research is short term; therefore, there is little time to focus on the reflective/reflexive process and subsequent benefits of classroom research, nor is there adequate time to formulate follow-up questions and continued research based on evidence from learners. Perhaps, most importantly, there is not a clear distinction made between the methodology of action research and its application to the unique setting of the classroom; however, this need not always be the case.

In one teacher education program, student teaching interns are taught the action research process in which they conduct and write up an inquiry project. They are then encouraged to carry out another action research inquiry in collaboration with their supervising teacher. This process promotes reflective conversation, often leads to team teaching, and helps build strong professional relationships. Only recently has action research been recognized as important to teacher preparation programs in which the success of the preservice and the student teacher is measured, in part, by their impact on the students they are teaching (Moore & Seeger, 2003; Shoyer & Yahnke, 2001; Wyatt, Meditz, Reeves, & Carr, 1999).

Meet Vicki and Jessica

Vicki mentored a student teacher, Jessica, for a full year in her fourth-grade open classroom located in a suburban school in a large school district in the Midwest. Together, they developed and conducted a classroom research project to study the advantages and disadvantages of using inquiry- and literature-based learning in teaching social studies. As part of her undergraduate requirement in teacher education, Jessica had completed an action research project the prior semester in Vicki's classroom. She knew the steps in the process but had never before had the opportunity to collaboratively conduct classroom research with another teacher or to apply the findings from her data analysis. Jessica remarked, "This was such an exciting process! I was truly able to see the utility of action research when working with Vicki to analyze data and make teaching choices. It also really helped me know what the students were thinking and learning. I will definitely take this skill with me into my own classroom!"

Vicki and Jessica studied the benefits of using inquiry- and literature-based instruction versus basal instruction to teach fourth-grade social studies. Their project lasted about eight weeks. The idea for this project resulted from Vicki's dissatisfaction with the district's newly adopted basal social studies textbook. She wanted to satisfy her hunch that students would learn more and be more motivated to learn if she incorporated inquiry- and literature-based instruction into daily lessons, using the textbook only as an alternate resource. Jessica was willing to help and learned first hand how to become, as she described, "a more thoughtful, reflective teacher." (Their complete project is included as Appendix B.)

In action classroom research, method and design must be uniquely suited to the reality of classroom problems and situations because research questions and data gathering become an integral part of daily lesson planning and assessment. This means that teachers must understand the components of the research process, learn to use them to their greatest benefit, and not consider them an extracurricular activity. The research design should be visible to the teacher in the daily lesson plan. The action research model offers teachers a methodological framework—a blueprint for design that, although formally introduced in a graduate or undergraduate teaching program, may be molded and utilized quite differently in the classroom.

Decisions about how to carry out, expand, and maintain the research process are contingent on the professional needs of the teacher as researcher. For example, initial action research questions may change or another data source may be added. You may find out what you needed to know two weeks into the project instead of three. Classroom research is not limited to the format of action research; however, it is useful to use this model as a springboard into broader frameworks of classroom research, like those introduced through the work of Cindy and Darlene in chapter 1.

Classroom research is teaching in the finest sense of the word. It is a process that empowers teachers to be learners on a daily, hourly basis rather than at the end of an artificially designated point in time typically associated with reports from dreaded standardized tests. And, its results are investigated through immediate classroom practice. The valuable knowledge teachers learn from the process, as well as the results of classroom research, must be supported and shared with other teachers and professionals if the research tradition is to grow strong. Reflective practice is a daily event for most teachers; however, having concrete evidence organized around pedagogical questions upon which to continuously reflect and act lends a new and empowering dimension to the teaching profession.

Chapter Summary

Action research as a method of classroom research is flexible. If the process of data collection is not working, change it. If your original research questions become far too obvious, modify them. Trust your instincts as a teacher and developing researcher as you move from the role of participant to observer and back again to discover the learning going on in your classroom.

Teachers who wish to make classroom research a part of their teaching and professional development will find that the methods and tools of action research open up new pathways to learning. In chapters 3 through 6, I will discuss the steps in the action research process in greater depth and provide examples and tips from practicing classroom teachers.

Conversation Starters . . .

- Brainstorm some classroom research topics with your colleagues. Why are these topics of interest to you? What do you hope to find out about them?

- Review the 12 steps to action research in this chapter. Where in your classroom do you follow some or all of these steps on a regular basis? Discuss what is missing and changes you might make to include these steps.

- With a colleague, review your weekly lesson plans. Explore potential data sources you are already using, and discuss ways in which you might use them to address a research topic.

Chapter 3

Nuts and Bolts of the Research Inquiry: Creating a Research Focus, Developing Background, Selecting Participants, and Writing Simple Questions

"What is the matter with Mary Jane?
She's crying with all her might and main,
And she won't eat her dinner— rice pudding again —
What is the matter with Mary Jane?"

(A. A. Milne, 1924)

Teacher research, like teaching, can be messy. It is an organic process fraught with human frailty that tugs at our beliefs while holding us accountable for our actions; the more we reflect on our discoveries from classroom inquiry, surprising or difficult as they may be, the more likely we will be to characterize our actions with the integrity of true professionals. I believe that if teachers are able to articulate a rationale for their teaching actions and the beliefs upon which they are based, then they will bring a new and powerful interdependence, definition, protocol, and professional integrity to both teaching and classroom research.

The following steps in action research for classroom teachers will help you organize an inquiry that will reveal information you most likely have never viewed in the same way before. The purpose of this process is to help you become a better teacher and to find new ways of expressing or defining your beliefs about teaching and learning.

Step 1. Identify a learning situation that is puzzling or interesting to you. This should be something you want or need to learn more about to inform your teaching.

Here you brainstorm the tough questions that crop up daily in your classroom. What have you been thinking about that puzzles you as a teacher? What teaching strategy have you wanted to try but were not sure how to monitor the results? What do I really know about the learning or behavior characteristics of a particular student? Some preliminary questions leading to research topics might be similar to those on the following list. Most are taken directly from conversations held prior to classroom research projects by elementary or middle school teachers.

- Why do some of my students do well in math but not in reading?

- How will the use of manipulatives in math influence learning in the intermediate grades?

- What assessment strategies seem to yield the best information about student learning in reading?

- What kinds of teaching strategies seem to work best in developing specific writing skills?

- What sort of background influences are affecting struggling readers and writers?

- What strategies support teaching vocabulary within literature circles?

- What are intermediate and middle school students' perceptions of the advantages and disadvantages of using inquiry- and literature-based learning?

- What steps are involved in establishing student ownership of performance-based rubrics?

- How does the knowledge students gain from developing their own rubrics transfer across content areas?

- In what ways does family involvement in authentic reading and writing opportunities affect students' enthusiasm toward reading and writing?

You will need to think of a sample teaching problem or focus. From this you will later craft specific research questions and find data sources to address them within the context of your own classroom. During this initial step of developing a research focus, it is helpful to think broadly while you brainstorm research ideas. Then, narrow your focus to a single problem or topic.

Organizing Your Ideas

If your brainstorming leads to a vast array of research topics, keep a list in your desk and create a time frame for addressing them. One way to organize for action research is to create your "lists" on large 5 x 8 in note cards so that as you think about your problem or focus, you can also begin to jot down potential classroom data sources. Write each idea on a separate card with a few key words and phrases to help you remember once you return to the card. You may later find that you have two related research problems that come together nicely to focus your classroom research inquiry. Next, prioritize your research ideas, thinking of your classroom schedule, available data sources, and professional time frames. (My sister, a mixed-media and watercolor artist, uses this sorting strategy to organize her multiple art projects. Some years ago, I expressed to her my frustration in organizing my research ideas and projects, so she offered this simple, reliable solution—which I have used ever since!)

Garnering Support and Building Collaboration for Classroom Research

Find out if other teachers have similar research interests, and support one another in designing and carrying out inquiry projects. This is an excellent way of building community in your school as well as establishing an atmosphere of support and mentoring. Show your principal your research cards and share your topics of interest. Your principal may have some to add! (In one elementary school, the principal not only volunteered to be a peer reviewer for several projects, but also expressed the desire to collaborate with one of the teachers on a project involving creative approaches to emergent literacy instruction.)

Share your research ideas with a colleague who might want to partner with you on conducting the research. Working with a partner often helps you view and validate data patterns from a different grade-level perspective. It is also a satisfying approach to building collegial professional relationships. The following vignette describes how two experienced teachers found a mutual research interest, developed research questions, brainstormed data sources, and helped one another through the entire process while still informing their own unique classroom settings.

Meet Janeen and Connie

Janeen and Connie were teacher colleagues who, for almost a year, had watched their school's new nature trail take shape. They both taught inquiry-based instruction and were eager to combine the teaching of science and writing in a natural setting (Bourne, 2000). Janeen taught kindergarten and Connie taught fifth grade in a small rural school in the Midwest. They wanted to find out if inquiry in a natural environment stimulated and focused student writing and multiage interactions about writing. To do so, they decided to study multiage buddy writing in an outdoor setting using science themes. This was their first formally recognized attempt at classroom research.

The data sources for these experienced teachers were typical anecdotal classroom assessments they ordinarily used in their classrooms: videotaped interactions between students and ongoing samples of the children's writing. In addition, they decided, that since this was a new multiage inquiry project, they would each keep a reflective teaching journal and compare responses as they progressed. While they had a hunch the project would be popular with both groups of children, they were able to:

1. document questions the children asked,

2. research student inquiries developing from the questions, and

3. discover ways in which the two grade levels approached the inquiries and the evolving roles of each of the "buddies."

As you might guess, Janeen and Connie anticipated that the fifth graders would guide the younger children; however, their tapes and reflective journals suggested this was not always true. A review of the conversations among student groups showed that the younger children were more curious and paid greater attention to small details than their older buddies.

News of the project spread rapidly through this small rural school and even into the community. Janeen and Connie informally shared what they had learned with parents and other teachers who began to think about ways they could utilize the nature trail as a learning setting. In addition, the district curriculum director requested that Janeen and Connie provide a district inservice presentation on multiage inquiry and writing based on their research findings.

Step 2.   Read a journal article or two about the topic, search the World Wide Web, or discuss it with a knowledgeable professional.

A busy classroom teacher may not have time or resources to conduct an extensive review of the literature addressing his or her research topic. For background information on your research topic, try reading a couple of journal articles, an interesting book on a new teaching strategy, or searching the World Wide Web, particularly Web sites established by such groups as the International Reading Association, National Council of Teachers of English, National Council of Teachers of Mathematics, National Council of Teachers of Social Studies or other established educational organizations. Vicki and Jessica utilized two educational Web sites for their background information. Following is an excerpt from their final project (Appendix B), which addresses what they found out to help them move forward with their inquiry.

> *"We used two Web sites to find background information on inquiry-based, literature-based learning. The first Web site details information that supports the use of inquiry-based learning, including a definition and how it differs from traditional classroom learning . . . These sites provided us with clear definitions of the two learning methodologies so that we were better able to focus our own reflective responses to the disadvantages and advantages of both."*

One note of caution about Internet sites: Beware of those that are not major organization affiliates or do not provide valid references to support their documents. Sometimes the information is inaccurate, disorganized, and/or lacking in sufficient theoretical grounding.

You may have recently attended a conference and are eager to try out a new strategy or program, but you are not sure how to assess its effectiveness, nor do you think you have quite enough background information to get started. The following example illustrates how action research may be useful in helping you begin.

Meet Glynis

Upon returning from a workshop on teaching algebra to the intermediate grades, Glynis was enthusiastic about trying out the new strategies she had learned. The workshop, *Making Alge-*

bra Child's Play (Borenson, 1999; Montney, 2000), focused on introducing algebra to the intermediate grades through math manipulatives coupled with reciprocal teaching (Palincsar & Brown, 1984). Although she had introduced algebraic concepts to her fifth graders previously, Glynis was discouraged with their learning responses. She decided to immediately move forward with the use of the new workshop strategies, monitoring the influence they had on student learning outcomes with an action research project. Since there were six other teachers in her building also conducting classroom research, she felt supported and ready to take the risk.

Glynis began her action research inquiry by reading two of the professional journal articles recommended by the workshop facilitator. These led her to formulate three major parts of her research design:

1. what to use for baseline data,

2. how she could include the entire class in her inquiry, and

3. tips on developing her own *Perceptions of Algebra Knowledge* survey (included in Appendix C along with her complete project).

The conference had helped her brush up on reciprocal teaching strategies in which students are invited to ask questions of the teacher and of themselves as learners (Palincsar & Brown, 1984). In addition, she returned from the conference armed with a kit of materials and valuable ideas about the kinds of inexpensive resources she could use as algebraic manipulatives.

There are many ways of brushing up on your knowledge. Background information should be acquired in a way that suits your learning style and preferences. It is surprising how much you glean from merely skimming a book and reading a selected chapter or two, seeking informal advice from colleagues who might have teaching experiences that relate to the research topic, or finding a video at your local university library to help you better understand your topic. All you need is enough knowledge to assist you in focusing on what is important to you as a teacher researcher as you design your inquiry project.

Of course, if you are writing a formal action research proposal for a university course, then a literature review is useful; but, for ongoing informal classroom research, your time is better spent in classroom data gathering and analysis to inform your specific teaching situation.

Meet Karen

Karen, an experienced reading specialist working in an inner city magnet school, was interested in the topic of Retrospective Miscue Analysis (RMA), which involves the reader in the analysis and discussion of his or her miscues (Goodman & Marek, 1996; Moore & Aspegren, 2001; Moore & Brantingham, 2001; 2003). She had used this strategy a few times with her resource room students and was beginning to see some interesting results. As one of her former graduate professors, Karen asked me to recommend some readings to help her focus her research topic. Later, we worked together to design and conduct an action research project with students in her resource room. Karen's purpose in conducting this inquiry was to inform her teaching and to demonstrate to other classroom teachers the effectiveness of using RMA strategies with these readers.

For Karen, initially exploring the inquiry approach to teaching and learning through the work of Goodman (1996) and Watson (1996) provided a foundation or "theoretical framework" for her studies. Reading a few chapters from these authors eventually led her to a journal article by Martens (1998), which yielded specific ideas for structuring her classroom research within her Title I classroom. Karen explains:

> *"These primary readings helped me to define the reasons I wanted to undertake each inquiry, rather than trying to artificially create a problem that did not exist for me or my students. This let me focus on what I was finding out from the inquiry rather than spending a lot of time trying to relate my students' results with various other studies and writings."*

Karen completed her first action research inquiry with a third-grade student, Nathan (pseudonym), on his understanding of "how reading works" through RMA. The heart of RMA involves empowering children to think about their reading, verbally question their reading responses, and inquire into the reading process—both theirs and others (Goodman, 1996). To do so, Karen, I, and Nathan discussed specific oral reading miscues he had made during a previously taped reading session as well as his retellings of text. This reader-response session is known as Retrospective Miscue Analysis (Aspegren & Moore, 2000; Goodman & Marek, 1996; Moore & Brantingham, 2003). Retrospective Miscue Analysis (RMA) typically involves the reader and a knowledgeable other, or a small group, in discussing reading miscues as well as retellings. Karen's primary readings in RMA helped her make decisions about how to set up her inquiry and to formulate questions to focus her project.

Step 3.   Decide which students will be participants in your research. This decision may be altered once you write your questions, but for now, envision what is most manageable for you in light of your research interest or need. Unless you plan to publish your research, you do not have to have parental permission; however, it's always a good idea to inform your principal of your plans.

In the next vignette, you will meet Greg, who was enrolled in the graduate course I taught in classroom research. He came to class with a specific student in mind. For this teacher, action research provided guidance in motivating a "puzzling" student to assume responsibility for more appropriate social behaviors.

Meet Greg

Greg, a fourth-grade teacher, was having difficulty managing a student who continually interrupted the classroom day with inappropriate behaviors, such as laughing unexpectedly or asking off-task questions. Worse, the child was also prone to dangerously aggressive behaviors with peers. To add to Greg's frustration, the student did not qualify for special services, so there was no support or plan in place to guide Greg's interactions with this puzzling youngster.

Greg decided to try three management strategies:

1. ignoring the behavior,

2   token economy, and

3   group points for this case study.

Token economy, in which Greg gave the student five pennies at the beginning of the school day, proved the most effective, both inside and outside the classroom. Each time the student showed inappropriate behavior, he gave Greg one of the pennies. At the end of the day, if the student had at least one penny left, he received a "token" reward, such as running errands, distributing classroom materials, or selecting a prize from the "Circle of Friends" box in Greg's classroom.

In studying the data from charts he had created to capture this student's behavior patterns, Greg realized that the token economy system changed this child's behavior both *inside and outside* the classroom, such as on the playground and in the school hallways. Other teachers remarked on these changes and reported them to Greg as well, thus indirectly involving other colleagues in his classroom research. The other teachers were surprised and impressed with the progress the student made in such a short period of time. They were also quite curious about Greg's research inquiry and design.

Most important, the information from his simple action research inquiry gave Greg new ideas about how to build similar strategies into his daily routines to continue to have teaching success with this child. Greg had learned that his case study student needed tangible ways of managing and representing his own behaviors. The student told Greg that this system was helping him feel better about himself as a member of the class.

Please note that Greg gathered quantitative (numerical) data through charting behavior responses, but he also took regular anecdotal records (qualitative data) to better describe the specifics of the student's attitude and responses. He blended the information from these sources to inform his teaching, which led to increased student responsibility and self-esteem as a class member.

Step 4.   Write two or three open-ended questions about your research problem or situation. Strive for questions to which you are fairly certain you will find answers or explanations.

It is helpful to think of writing research questions like writing lesson plans. You will most likely be asking questions that focus on your instructional objectives. In the next inquiry, you will hear from a teacher who was interested in verifying the results of a highly touted writing program. Many teachers liked the program and said it was "effective," but Linda questioned the influence of the new program on the writing organization of her students.

Meet Linda

Linda, a second-grade teacher, wanted to find out if the program, Powerful Writing (Treat, 2001), recently adopted by her district to support their school improvement plan, was indeed developing her students' organizational writing strategies in addition to increasing their appropriate use of transition words. These were two areas with which her entire class struggled. Linda's research questions were:

1. How will the implementation of the Powerful Writing (2001) program change the organization of students' writing?

2. What effect will this program have on students' use of transition words?

Simple, open-ended questions helped Linda focus her data. She found some very specific information as she looked for answers to the research questions in student writings. Sharing the results of this inquiry with a group of preservice teachers and university faculty, she noted:

"I found Powerful Writing provides me with a visual tool that helps students write their thoughts in an organized manner. Depending on the type of writing, it also lends itself to the use of transition words, but Powerful Writing alone does not elicit the use of transitions. This graphic organizer strategy works to support the use of transition words when coupled with lists of words that students, or teachers and students, have brainstormed earlier."

Specific and insightful answers to Linda's classroom research questions informed her continued use of the writing program in ways that better met the learning needs of her students.

Writing Research Questions

Research questions are like writing the perfect reminders to ourselves. One of my preservice teachers once remarked, "They're a lot like writing lesson objectives," in that they keep our research on track. We know where we started, and through our evidence, we assess for patterns of information that will help us answer our questions. Research questions are not set in stone, as some empiricists would have us believe. They are flexible and must conform to the dynamic of our particular classroom setting. Seldom does a teacher start a classroom action research project and end it with questions that are worded exactly the same as those at the beginning of the inquiry. Experience has taught me that this does not detract from the reliability and validity of the results; in fact, it enhances overall credibility and makes the information from the inquiry immediately useful. The case which follows demonstrates how simple it is to refocus and reframe research questions.

Meet Marilee

Marilee, a fourth-grade teacher, had just finished a classroom research project built on the action research model. At first, her questions included the influence of reader-selected miscue analysis (Watson, 1996), reciprocal teaching, and direct instruction on comprehension. These were far too broad and unfocused to be useful to her teaching. The miscue analysis inquiry was put on hold, as Marilee decided to narrow her focus to the influence of Reciprocal Teaching (Palincsar & Brown, 1984) and Direct Explanation (Duffy, Roehler, & Herrmann, 1988) on the comprehension of a group of 10 students of mixed ability levels in her classroom. Reciprocal Teaching (1984) involves students and teachers asking questions of one another after reading. Direct Explanation (1988) is using visual imagery and story grammar to understand context and guide comprehension (Burrow, 2001). Her research questions were:

1. How will Reciprocal Teaching (1984) coupled with Direct Explanation (1988) affect reading accuracy and comprehension?
2. In what ways will Reciprocal Teaching (1984) coupled with Direct Explanation (1988) affect lower-achieving readers versus average-achieving readers?
3. What cognitive behaviors do these strategies bring out in learner response?

Marilee chose to conduct pre and post informal reading inventories to measure growth in the students' reading comprehension related to her inquiry. While these scores did not increase a great deal, her open-ended, topic-focused research questions enabled her to articulate other kinds of progress that she believed were just as important. This included, but was not limited to, the students' growing skills in asking and answering higher-level questions during reading workshop. Questions 2 and 3 helped her capture the implications she was seeing in the student responses.

Chapter Summary

In this chapter, you learned the first four steps toward designing an action research inquiry:

1. creating a research focus or topic,

2. developing background knowledge,

3. selecting participants or research samples, and

4. writing research questions.

These first four steps "set up" the action research inquiry. It is important to the organization of your inquiry that they be developed before you move on to the next stage; however, you may later decide to make changes along the way. Much like a lesson plan, your action research project should be flexible as you decide how it works best for you. For example, early in the process you may need to adjust a research question or change a data source in order for the information you are gathering to be of optimal value to your research focus. Simply note the changes and keep going.

Conversation Starters . . .

- Develop two questions that you might ask, focused on a topic you think you may be interested in researching. With a partner, describe and discuss the learners in your classroom and determine how you might structure your inquiry—as a single case study, as a focus group, or with the entire class as participants.

- Find out the procedures your principal might ask you to follow as you conduct your inquiry: Will parental permission need to be secured? Will you be able to share your inquiry progress with others at faculty meetings, or during outside support groups' times? When and where will you be inviting your principal or building administrator into your classroom to share the progress of your inquiry?

- Brainstorm a list of resource personnel who might provide background knowledge or be able to suggest some readings that will help you better understand your research topic and the data that may come from your project.

Chapter 4

Research Does Not Have to Be an Extracurricular Assignment: Discovering the Data Sources in Your Classroom

"I like talking to Rabbit. He talks about sensible things.
He doesn't use long, difficult words, like Owl. He uses
short, easy words, like 'What about lunch?'"

(A. A. Milne, 1928)

Step 5. Reexamine your research questions and determine where you can find evidence to address them. It is advisable to have at least two data sources for each question; however, these may overlap. Then, you are ready to determine what you might use for baseline data, sometimes called pre and post assessment information.

To keep your inquiry from becoming an "extracurricular activity," look for existing data sources in your classroom, examining your daily instruction for "evidence" of learning. These might be assignments that you think will address your research questions, writing samples, or other daily assignments in which students solve problems dealing with specific content or subject matter. Other potential data sources include: integrated content projects, student journals, teacher-made tests or surveys, content-specific projects, a teaching journal, anecdotal records, videotaped lessons, or jotted notes on lesson plans as reminders of what did or did not go well.

It is advisable to have at least two data sources per question for comparison and verification purposes when you are ready to analyze the data. If you wish to publish or present your study formally, particularly if you are investigating questions related to teacher accountability, you need to have at least three data sources per question to "triangulate," or compare, the responses among sources (you will learn more about this in chapter 6). This recommendation is in keeping with recognized guidelines for analyzing qualitative data in education (Bogdan & Biklen, 1992).

As stated, data sources may be readily available through existing assignments; however, do not hesitate to modify assignments to ensure adequate data are collected. If you are implementing a new strategy or program, then you may also need to modify assignments and routines to support the new materials and procedures.

You might recall that Vicki and Jessica examined the influence of literature-based instruction on social studies learning versus the use of a basal text (Appendix B). Among their data sources were authentic student work samples, teacher reflections, and student attitude surveys. Data sources reflect the learning events and outcomes present in your classroom. It is important to always consider which of these outcomes (often student work samples) will most adequately address your research questions.

Where to Look

Begin by taking notes in an organizer for about a week like that of Figure 4.1 (also included in Appendix A). Observe, listen, and look for assignments and responses to teaching and learning that give you authentic information about the students. Just a plain notebook and a few simple headings like those in Figure 4.1 will enable you to view your classroom differently. Decide from your organizer what classroom learning event (i.e., activities, workshops, practice of strategies) will yield at least two sources of reliable data to address each research question.

Figure 4.1. Organizer for identifying classroom data sources.

Date	Learning Event	Research Question Addressed
2/6	Writing Workshop (peer editing)	How can students develop individual spelling lists during writing workshop?
2/9	Writing Workshop (writing drafts)	How can students develop individual spelling lists during writing workshop?
2/12	Writing Workshop (direct minilesson)	Where can I most effectively connect phonics to writing in daily work?

After you have identified data sources, be certain these events will yield tangible evidence of student learning. We know that every good lesson includes some form of assessment which yields such evidence. For example, on 2/12 of Figure 4.1 the teacher decided that minilessons during writing workshop and small group discussions provided two data sources that addressed how she could most effectively connect writing and phonics instruction. However, she needed some way of *assessing* the influence of minilessons and group discussion on phonics skill development when those strategies were used. She decided:

1   use the writing samples which follow the minilesson to determine where the phonics skill is successfully implemented in the students' writing, and

2   in some organized fashion, ask the children to maintain questions related to spelling as well as content in their small groups.

Keeping the questions in group folders is recommended.

Whether studying student behaviors or learning, the data source should be characterized by authentic response—whether it's verbal, nonverbal, or written. The same concept is true if you are trying to improve some aspect of your teaching, such as your skill in questioning. For example, student responses to you, your responses to students (recorded on videotape, audiotape, or work samples) serve as rich, authentic data sources for this research inquiry. Using an authentic classroom response as a data source, instead of for example, a standardized test, validates your research focus and outcomes. It lends credence to your ability as a teacher and a researcher to carefully make instructional decisions based on response data that is immediately relevant to your classroom. You may capture and analyze the data quantitatively (numerically), or qualitatively (anecdotally), but the authenticity of your data as related to your classroom situation remains the same. Depending on you research project, you may also utilize existing archived data, such as test scores or school improvement plan reports, to compare and contrast your findings—but the authenticity of your own classroom research is, by far, the most relevant.

If you are trying out a new teaching strategy or program, you may have to rework class assignments to match the objectives of the strategy or program. This is what we do as teachers, regardless of whether the implementation of the new material will be monitored by a classroom research plan and process. The difference is how you organize and view the data. In classroom research, teachers examine learning outcomes against focused research questions. Their findings will eventually emerge as patterns of learning, behavior, or teaching—thus providing sound evidence to inform instructional decision making.

Collecting Baseline Data

Since your baseline data may be your first set of data responses, it is important to determine your data sources first. However, a simple assessment prior to data collection, followed by the same assessment at the end of your inquiry, also works in establishing a baseline of comparison. In brief, baseline data may be a simple, informal pre and post assessment, your own documented observations, or a more formal measure of a learning objective. Baseline data is intended to give you a point of comparison—a means of determining change. In classroom research, the teacher then determines whether or not this change is significant, based on his or her understanding of the situation and the variables involved.

It is helpful to have a rubric that captures or highlights the baseline performance of the student or students in your classroom inquiry. This is a very simple process, but establishing a baseline does assist you when it's time to analyze your findings. Patterns of learner response, and possibly, changes in learning performance, will be more readily discernable. Glynis, the fifth-grade teacher who was exploring new strategies for teaching algebraic concepts, describes how she collected her baseline data:

> *I gave the students a teacher-made algebra pretest. Out of 21 students, 20 failed it. They completed 0–2 problems correctly. The one child who scored 6 out of 10 had some exposure to algebra in fourth grade at another school. The students were also given a survey to record their feeling about "algebra" before lessons were taught and after they had exposure to the lessons of the new approach. I found that most children had heard the term "algebra" before, and knew that letters were used with numbers, but that was the extent of their "pre" knowledge.*

The baseline-data process Glynis chose proved very helpful in her final analysis of data, but sometimes, as Marilee (chapter 3) discovered, you may later need to look at other "baseline" information as the results of your inquiry unfold. Said differently, classroom research which focuses on something very specific may also point to the discrete, even unnoticed patterns of learning. As teacher researchers, we must remain open to all the possibilities.

You met Marilee in the previous chapter. Marilee learned that while student scores remained about the same on her pre and post informal reading inventory measures (baseline data), other developments that could only be documented through student performance and her own observations (two data sources) were taking place. She explained:

> *I observed students grow in their ability to apply reading strategies and I did not feel like the informal reading baseline data adequately addressed this aspect of their base knowledge, or their learning. For example, at the beginning of the inquiry, students asked questions such as, "In what town did the character live?" Later, students began asking questions such as, "What was this poem mainly about?" or, "What were the characters really talking about?"*

To help her compare student responses prior to the inquiry, Marilee scrutinized her own anecdotal records to contrast what she had observed early in the inquiry with what she was later observing. This baseline was far more revealing than the baseline provided by the informal reading inventory scores. Classroom research is fluid and sometimes, like teaching, a little messy. It is only useful if it yields information meaningful to teaching and learning.

Step 6. Determine the time frame and procedure you will use to collect data. First, collect your baseline data, then develop and implement a procedure for gathering and organizing the rest of the data that fits into your classroom routine. For some projects, it may be necessary to garner parental permission, while for others the classroom research is imbedded into the daily instructional plan.

Establishing your baseline and keeping track of the rest of your research data is imperative to the success of your project. You may remember Greg who sought to motivate and change the inappropriate behaviors of one of his students. He recorded the number of acceptable responses from this student on four separate charts. During this four-week inquiry, the daily classroom routine remained fairly consistent. Greg devised an "in-class" anecdotal record sheet as well as an "out-of-class anecdotal record sheet," in which he recorded student responses and situations (see Figure 4.2). In addition, he developed charts to monitor student responses to different kinds of management strategies. These two charts included an "in-class" quantitative data chart, as well as an "out-of-class" quantitative data chart (see Figure 4.3).

Figure 4.2. Sample entries for Greg's "in-class" anecdotal record chart.

Date/Strategy/Day	Anecdotal Notes and Times
3–8 Baseline (Friday)	Inappropriate behaviors at desk (10:45 a.m.); Talking to others (11:40 a.m.); Sudden outburst during math lesson (1:00 p.m.)
3–25 Ignore (Monday)	Loud talking during morning work session (8:45 a.m.); Talking during SSR time—disrupting other students (9:15 a.m.)
4–01–02 Token Economy (Monday)	Shouting out answers inappropriately (10:45 a.m.)
4–02–02 Token Economy (Tuesday)	Insulting others during morning activity (9:55 a.m.)

Figure 4.3. Behavior/response data collected by Greg over a four-week period.

Date/Day of Week	Strategy	Counted Behaviors Per Day
3–08–02 (F)	Baseline (no strategy)	4
3–11–02 (M)	Baseline	4
3–12–02 (T)	Baseline	3
3–13–02 (W)	Baseline	6
3–14–02 (TH)	Baseline	7
3–25–02 (M)	IGNORE	3
3–26–02 (T)	IGNORE	5
3–27–02 (W)	IGNORE	3
3–28–02 (TH)	IGNORE	3
3–29–02 (F)	IGNORE	4
4–01–02 (M)	TOKEN ECONOMY	1
4–02–02 (T)	TOKEN ECONOMY	2
4–03–02 (W)	TOKEN ECONOMY	2
4–04–02 (TH)	TOKEN ECONOMY	3
4–05–02 (F)	TOKEN ECONOMY	2
4–08–02 (M)	GROUP POINT SYSTEM	2
4–09–02 (T)	GROUP POINT SYSTEM	2
4–10–02 (W)	GROUP POINT SYSTEM	3
4–11–02 (TH)	GROUP POINT SYSTEM	2
4–12-02 (F)	GROUP POINT SYSTEM	2

Definitions of Strategies

Ignore: During classroom instruction, the teacher totally ignored all targeted behaviors displayed by the student.

Token Economy: The student was given five pennies at the beginning of each school day. Upon displaying the targeted behavior, the student would hand one penny to the teacher. If the student still had one penny at the end of the school day, he was given a reward.

Group Point System: During the school day, students were split into groups and placed in classroom pods. Each group would be given points for high test scores, appropriate behavior, and aiding the classroom teacher. Points were subtracted for late assignments, inappropriate behavior inside as well as outside the classroom.

Without question, classroom research, like teaching, requires organization as you examine existing schedules and routines for appropriate data-gathering opportunities, then decide how to organize the data-gathering process.

Creating a Visual Time Frame or Data Calendar

When organizing your data-gathering time frame, it is useful to have some sort of visual reminder to which you can easily refer. For example, Cindy's colleagues were impressed with the calendar she set up for data gathering, but, upon closer examination, realized that it was a computer-generated calendar in which she had carefully coordinated her data gathering and analysis with her instructional time within a typical week.

As you learned in chapter 1, Cindy was no stranger to classroom research; therefore, she understood the importance of folding typical instruction into classroom-research procedures. As a part of one of many research inquiries, she investigated three new comprehension strategies to use with first graders; therefore, on specific dates and times during the week she incorporated the teaching and practice of the new comprehension strategies into her daily schedule. How well the children were able to apply the strategies to various assignments provided her with sufficient data (evidence) for her classroom action research project without "adding to" her already full schedule.

There are other variations on this practice, as you will see in the next plan for studying the phonemic awareness patterns of development in a kindergarten classroom.

Meet Christy

Christy's inquiry focused on phonemic awareness patterns of her 23 second-semester kindergarten students. She planned her data gathering according to what the students did each week, adding nothing extra to her already busy day. An excerpt from her plan may be viewed in Figure 4.4, in which she identified data sources within existing instructional practices. These included:

1. student journals,

2. a letter/sound assessment during animated literacy,

3. a phonemic awareness assessment during animated literacy,

4. a reading and writing rubric scale from literacy centers, and

5. her anecdotal records. Her first set of data responses served as her baseline of information.

Figure 4.4. Christy's plan of organization.

Plan of Organization: March 25–May 3
Phonemic Awareness Inquiry

Week 1: March 25–29, 2002
Journal 3 times a week.
Daily/weekly animated literacy activities.
Literacy Center: Sound recognition through dino-phonics game.

Week 2: April 1–5, 2002
Journal 3 times a week.
Daily/weekly animated literacy activities.
Literacy Center: Sound recognition through sound tubs/ also when Mrs. White says a sound, write that letter on the dry erase board (beginning sounds).

Week 3: April 8–12, 2002
Journal 3 times a week.
Daily/weekly animated literacy activities.
Literacy Center: Sound substitution with animated literacy songs and dry erase boards for review of beginning sounds and writing words.

If you recall, Marilee was interested in the influence of Reciprocal Teaching (Palincsar & Brown, 1984) and Direct Explanation (Duffy, Roehler, & Herrmann, 1988) on comprehension. She organized the classroom reading routine and schedule to include these two strategies. Since Marilee's research inquiry was one which she plans to later publish, she sought written permission from students and parents as well as her school administration. If, like Marilee, you plan to publish your work or share it at a conference as a more formal research study, you should let your students and their parents know what you are doing and why, then obtain their written permission prior to the study. Be sure to explain that the purpose of the research is to improve classroom learning.

When you are conducting the research within the context of normal instruction for purposes of improving a teaching strategy or assessing student learning, it is not necessary to obtain permission. However, obtaining permissions, or simply explaining your research project to parents, demonstrates your professionalism and interest in the improvement of instruction and learning. Share your findings with interested parents. Marilee shared her inquiry results with a number of parents who were pleased with the questions and responses of their children. Also, when Marilee informally shared selected responses and data, she authentically demonstrated how reciprocal teaching might be extended at home as a part of a homework assignment or in general conversation.

What Real Teacher Has Time for Any of This Stuff?

A preservice teacher once asked me, "What real teacher has time for any of this stuff?" (Moore, 1996). We had been discussing how to set up an action research inquiry, and I suggested keeping a field journal as one data source to compare teaching actions with outcomes from student assignments. The preservice teacher's resistance was to keeping the field journal and he may have had a valid point. If the data source is not going to work for you, then choose an alternative. While field journals are valuable to most, it is fruitless to design the perfect research project, then find that you are overwhelmed or discouraged by one or more aspects of the data-collection process. Journaling is not for everyone.

After some deliberation, I suggested, instead of journaling, that the preservice teacher compare his lesson plans and reflective notes on the results of the lesson to actual learning outcomes on student assignments associated with the lessons. (It made me think that all of us as teachers could benefit from this practice, as well.) This alternative proved quite successful. The preservice teacher was not focused on finding time for journaling; rather, he was focused on his teaching and student learning. By comparing the students' responses to what he had hoped to teach, he was able to easily pinpoint the areas he needed to reteach. He also was able to examine his teaching strategies to determine which ones were more consistently effective in supporting student learning.

Integral to conducting classroom research is using existing instructional tools and time lines for organizing, examining, and utilizing the rich data of daily learner response. Once organized into the everyday routine, classroom research becomes a powerful asset to daily teaching and learning. It invites us to ask questions we might never have thought of before and demonstrates teaching or learning patterns we might not otherwise have seen. It is not limited to time or situation; rather, it is a continuous assessment of patterns of learner response.

Keep in mind that you are the one in charge of making the decisions about data gathering and how you will analyze it. As you revisit your research problem and questions, view the teaching processes and tools of your existing classroom routine from the perspective of your research questions. Then decide how to capture the data. You can construct your own observation sheets or make use of the many that are already published or found online. Following is an example of one teacher's use of an anecdotal record-keeping sheet focused on teacher and learner response.

Meet Kelli

Kelli, a third-grade teacher, explored the use of anecdotal records to help her collect and organize data. She used a Form I developed to assist her in better understanding the relationship between teacher and learner response (see Figure 4.5). A blank form for this record-keeping tool may be viewed in Appendix A; another variation of the same form may be found in Appendix B.

Kelli was interested in learning more about Brandon (pseudonym), a third-grade student whose responses were minimal, both in conversation and writing. In sharing her project with others, she said:

After taking anecdotal notes on the interactions Brandon and I had, I found that he really responds and works best when he is in small groups . . . He seems to feed off the other students' energy or response and shares ideas and questions more freely. My 'aha' moment with Brandon, after reading my records, was that not even one-on-one did he do as well as he did in smaller groups—an assumption I had erroneously made for some time.

Figure 4.5 is a chart used to sort and categorize learner and teacher interaction. This was the research tool that Kelli used to gather information to help her decide how to best assist Brandon with his reading comprehension. The entries below are similar to previous entries that show Brandon functions best in a small group setting where he reads with others.

Figure 4.5. Kelli's anecdotal record summary.

Date	Learning Event	Teacher's Action	Student Response	Teacher Response	Evaluation of Interaction
3/28	Small group oral reading	Asked questions during reading	Brandon answered all questions accurately, even inferential	Praise, more questions	Brandon was more comfortable and confident than I'd ever seen him
4/4	Independent reading of biography	Asked students to write important events/dates while they read	Brandon found important facts sometimes but was struggling	Took him through the story using smaller step by step and sentence by sentence	Very difficult for him. Needed help through the entire reading.

Chapter Summary

In this chapter, various kinds of data sources were introduced, particularly those that may be derived from existing assignments or classroom projects; these are authentic responses to teaching and learning. Identifying rich data sources for an action research inquiry will strengthen your skill in building a variety of application and assessment strategies into your overall instructional planning and teaching.

Conversation Starters . . .

- Think of a new teaching strategy you would like to try. What kinds of data sources might provide evidence of student learning as a result of the implementation of the new strategy?

- Using the chart provided in Figure 4.1, spend a few minutes this week locating potential data sources for your research questions. Share these with a friend.

- Describe your classroom routine to another person along with your research questions. What data sources does he or she point out?

Chapter 5

Sorting and Coding: Setting the Stage for Greater Discoveries

"He who never made a mistake, never made a discovery."

(Samuel Smiles)

Step 7. Continue to collect data over a three- to six-week period of time, coding it as you collect. It is likely you will change some of your coding decisions as you make greater discoveries.

By now, you have identified data sources, established a baseline, and have outlined a data-collection process. It is now time to begin coding the data—usually during the second week of the inquiry. This is one of the most enjoyable aspects of action research; it is the beginning of new discoveries about teaching and learning. The process is simple: You sort individual pieces of data to the research questions to which they seem most relevant. Sometimes there is overlap and one piece of data (evidence) addresses more than one question, particularly if you are working with writing samples or other kinds of student assignments. As you sort, you will begin to see patterns emerge. Eventually, you will assign categories or themes to these patterns.

Be sure you have sufficient and appropriate data. Begin by informally reading or reviewing the responses in each of the data sources the first week into the inquiry. Do the data really address your research questions? If after the second week they do, then there is probably no need to adjust your sources; however, if there is a mismatch between data and questions, then adjust your sources or change your questions—whichever suits your research needs and interests. It is important to have enough data to identify patterns of learner response. If you have fewer than five responses coded to a question, you might want to consider rewording the question, developing an alternative question, or simply changing your data source. It is also possible that the question might be better suited to another inquiry at another time. Remember, the whole point of classroom research is to gather sufficient evidence to inform teaching and support student learning.

Coding the Data

There are various ways of coding the data; however, color coding is one way of sorting descriptive or anecdotal data, which I highly recommend (Bogdan & Biklen, 1992), particularly to novice researchers. It is highly visible and easily summarized later into categories or themes. Other processes used by teachers are sorting data by type into folders, condensing data into short pie-graph summaries, or just making and sorting lists of commonalities and differences. One process is superior to another only if it better helps you to focus the data. Most important: Make time for regular data analysis from the beginning to the end of the inquiry. While you may not change your teaching until you are ready to stop collecting data, you can begin to think about the data responses that are emerging and consider ways you can use that information to support student learning.

Color Coding

As you collect data, you may wish to use a simple color-coding technique to keep it organized. To do this, read the data and color code (highlight) it according to your research questions. For example, all green highlights are coded to question one, all yellow highlights are responses to question two. This helps you manage the data on a regular basis. Organize your time to do this *at least* weekly.

To realize how simple it is to color code data, examine the following excerpt from Marilee's anecdotal records, which if you recall from chapter 3, served as one of her data sources. As you can see, she readily captured cognitive behaviors associated with either Reciprocal Teaching (1984) or Direct Explanation (1988). Her research questions with the colors she assigned to them are listed in figure 5.1. She then highlighted information in her data sources related to the specific questions by color—like those of her anecdotal records in Figure 5.2. The result of this process is a color-coded text in which you can easily *see* and then *sort* the items that inform each research question.

Figure 5.1. Marilee's research questions by color.

1. How will Reciprocal Teaching (1984) coupled with Direct Explanation (1988) affect reading accuracy and comprehension? (green)

2. In what ways will Reciprocal Teaching (1984) coupled with Direct Explanation (1988) affect lower-achieving readers versus average-achieving readers? (yellow)

3. What cognitive behaviors do these strategies bring out in learner response? (blue)

Figure 5.2. Samples from Marilee's anecdotal records sorted to the research questions.

March 10:   I was beginning to think we were stuck on literal-level questions, but today was a breakthrough. The kids really got into a good discussion about kinds of good and bad. If you cannot pay your taxes, is that always "bad" or "your fault" and why. (blue)

March 13:   I think I am starting to better understand direct explanation as a strategy that is okay with both groups of children as long as I am really sure they are with me. I notice the lower group seems to need both strategies at once in order to give responses that show they are understanding the reading. Joy said today that, "Asking questions helps me see how things fit together." (yellow)

March 17:   I'm beginning to see the value not only in checking comprehension but in asking the children the kinds of questions they might ask if they really wanted to help someone understand the material better. (blue)

Next, if you are working with descriptive data, such as anecdotal records and student work samples, review your color coding, then summarize your notes (main ideas) under each question. Marilee made copies of the student responses, color coded them to her questions, then cut the data into sections, placing them into folders on which she had written the research questions. Some teachers prefer to read each color-grouped set of data and summarize the responses weekly in short bulleted lists. Remember, you should by the end of your inquiry have at least five responses coded to each question. This does not necessarily mean five discrete pieces of data per question, although that is most common. Sometimes there is more than one piece of evidence embedded in a learner's response. For example, if you are studying rate and accuracy during daily problem-solving sessions, you may see improvement in both on a single assignment.

The key is to synthesize your data but to not overlook anything important. View each learner response as potential evidence of some aspect related to the research questions/topics, and later, you will look for categories or themes.

Perhaps the most common problem in collecting the data is not maintaining it in an organized fashion so that it is easily coded to the research question. Develop a chart or rubric that helps you keep track of various data sources, such as the one in figure 5.3. Stacy was studying Powerful Writing (Treat, 2001). Following is an organizational tool for documenting one of her data sources: student writing samples. Later, the results were coded to her research question about the influence of Powerful Writing (2001) on organization in writing.

Figure 5.3. Rubric for studying the writing trait of *organization*.

Student	Baseline Data	Season	Sport	Choice	Essay
A	2	4	3	4	3
B	2	3	3	5	4
C	2	3	2	4	4
D	2	2	3	2	3
E	2	2	2	3	3
F	2	3	3	2	4

Other Coding Strategies

As stated, there are various ways of coding. The color-coding process may not be suitable for all action research studies, particularly if you are working with largely quantifiable data (numerical) rather than descriptive or anecdotal data. If you want to see patterns of student improvement using a specific assessment tool, then perhaps a system similar to what the following teachers worked out might be helpful.

Meet Audra and Lori

Audra teaches second grade in a large suburban school. To satisfy her own professional development questions, she studied the effects of cross-age tutoring on the attitude and reading comprehension of second graders who are tutored by fourth-grade buddies. Her project was completed in coordination with Lori, a fourth-grade teacher with similar interests at the same school. After establishing a baseline from existing scores, their continuing data consisted of daily pre and post reading scores to assess the effect of the buddy reading sessions on context, fact, inference, conclusion, and sequence skills. To assess attitude, they conducted a pre and post *Reading Attitude Survey* (McKenna & Kear, 1990) on each second grader.

Audra explains how she and Lori organized and coded the data:

> We recorded scores for each pre and post test by using a class roster. We put a column for the pre test comprehension scores in red and a column for post test scores in black. In a third column, we listed attitude pre and post scores in blue. We then created a second chart, utilizing the roster. If a student improved during our project, we marked their name with a plus sign (+); if the student declined, we posted a minus sign (–); or if a student's scores sustained, we posted a slash sign (/).

For Audra and Lori, color coding was not the preferred method, so they worked out another simple, but efficient plan for coding the data that better suited the intent of their inquiry. Nothing extra was added to their typical day; instead, they reorganized reading times so that the two age groups could read together.

Step 8. At the end of your designated time frame, reread your coded data and see if you still agree with your coding decisions. Modify them as needed. Ask a trusted colleague or your principal to review your coding and offer feedback. To provide continuous verification and feedback on coding, teachers often form support groups comprised of teachers in the local building or district who are conducting action research projects.

Obtaining feedback from others:
"The best mirror is a friend's eye." (Goethe)

After you have started coding your data, ask two or more of your colleagues to interpret your findings through their various perspectives. This is best done through study groups. In one of the professional development school sites, I worked with three groups of teachers who met once every two weeks after school to critique their inquiry procedures and data analysis. Several said that this process helped answer questions about their projects and to guide the data coding. Asking others to verify your procedures and coding is useful, since they may interpret information in ways that you might not have considered. *Please understand that you are not requesting a formal analysis.* You are simply asking them to read portions of your data and to see if your rationale for coding makes sense to them as teachers.

One fourth-grade teacher, Stacy, who you met earlier in the chapter, explains how important her peer reviewer's advice was in helping her see all aspects of her inquiry.

> Connie's review made me look at how important my writing trait scores were in my findings. I was reluctant because some of the kids showed inconsistencies on their scores. We decided that this is just a true example of how it is in class. Kids change from day to day because of mood, lack of sleep, interest, and more. The final results are what you get from them at that given time as they demonstrate what they know.

Peer review is also an excellent venue for introducing a novice teacher or student teacher to action research. In addition, you establish a mentoring relationship based on a common topic or interest, as did Vicki and her student teacher, Jessica, who you met in chapter 2. Shared information and processes are vital to the success of action research in your building or even in your own classroom. It can, and should be, a social process from which conversations about learning begin to flourish.

Vicki and Jessica created a T-Chart to regularly compare their reflective responses to their inquiry about the differences between inquiry-based instruction and basal instruction in a social studies unit. The following excerpt, Figure 5.4, comes from one of Jessica's T-Chart entries. A blank form for the chart may be found in Appendix A.

Figure 5.4. Jessica's reflective written response T-Chart.

Basal Instruction versus Inquiry: Advantages for Teachers and Students	
Basal Instruction	**Inquiry- and Literature-Based Instruction**
Text and materials are laid out for the teacher to follow.	Using authentic text allows students to see cultures, regions, concepts, etc. from the point of view of those involved.
All of the material is in one place.	Researching, group projects, and picture books hold students' interest much longer.
Students have access to text and pictures.	Students feel free to pursue their interests and find answers to their questions.
	Students stay actively engaged in the learning.
	Students bring to class stories and objects related to the unit.
	Students seek out a variety of resources, including family members, Internet, public and school libraries, books, encyclopedias, and each other!
	Easy to integrate information from the unit across the curriculum and make many personal, text, and world connections.

Disadvantages/Advantages for Teachers and Students

Basal Instruction	Inquiry- and Literature-Based Instruction
Little or no opportunity to pursue students' interests.	Nothing is laid out for the teacher; a lot of work and research goes into a unit taught this way.
Students usually find the text difficult to understand, follow, and enjoy.	More time-consuming to assess student progress when it doesn't consist of only worksheets.
Very little information about numerous topics.	

Student Perspectives on Coded Data

Here's another idea for acquiring a fresh perspective on your data coding: Ask your students to help with the verification process. Decide which aspect of the data you want them to review, and then create a list of questions or a simple rubric that easily captures their responses. For example, you may wonder if your perceptions of their attitude toward a particular learning tool are accurate, based on your anecdotal records. Share some of your notes and ask them for interpretive feedback. Often their interpretation of data is different from ours, based on what was happening in their lives that particular day.

Debbie, introduced in chapter 1, was studying the process of student-developed performance presentation rubrics. As she coded their responses to the use of the rubric, she found they were much more attentive to completing the project carefully, using more resources and organizational skill than in previous projects. A classroom survey of her students verified her coding, also letting her see more specific reactions of individual students to the student-generated rubric process and outcomes.

You do not have to present all of the data to your students; merely sample bits and pieces of which you are somewhat unsure or curious. This works well with authentic data samples, such as student writing, journal entries, responses to essay questions, and other descriptive data. You might explain to them that you have reviewed their final drafts of a writing project in which you were looking for connections they made to a particular topic. Show specific students your color-coded data from their individual papers and ask them to comment on the accuracy. Were you able to find and interpret all the connections they made? This is a procedure easily worked into a writing conference between teacher and student.

If you are charting comprehension responses, you might ask students to verify differing points of view on main ideas, characters, theme, and other concepts that present multiple perspectives. They will appreciate becoming a part of the process, but perhaps more importantly, they become engaged in a thoughtful, reflective response process which models how we want students to perceive and think about their own learning. This is also another way of integrating your classroom research into instructional time and supporting learning through your findings and those of your students. In this situation, classroom research, teaching, and learning truly become reciprocal processes.

Common Pitfalls in Data Coding

The most common pitfall in the initial coding process is trying to code too much of the data to the questions at once. Compare this to trying to grade every single paper or activity. You are looking for kernels of understanding; there is no need to high-light every piece of the data; decide on the assignments you want to code from your data source. For example, if you are using data from literacy centers, code only data from designated days, not daily. You want to keep your coding simple so that it is not bur-densome to your schedule; rather, it becomes a helpful tool in assessment. Stacy, the fourth-grade teacher who was studying her students' use of organization in their writing, reiterates my advice:

> *After talking with my peer reviewer, Connie, I realized that I had coded more than I needed for summarizing my in-formation. It's hard to leave some of the trivial things out, but now that I've done it, I would know next time how to alleviate some of the repetitious coding I did.*

A second pitfall is trying to analyze your findings too early. Code the data a few at a time and simply reflect on what you are finding, keeping an open mind that things may change, given more time for students to benefit from whatever modifications or strategies you are monitoring through your research. Another pitfall is procrastination—waiting until the end of the time you have allotted to your inquiry to code the data. Plan to begin cod-ing after you garner your first week of data and no later than your second week. This gives you practice and skill that will grow over the rest of your project as well giving you insight on whether your data sources will yield sufficient evidence to inform your inquiry.

Chapter Summary

In this chapter, you are encouraged to sort and analyze your data by looking at learner responses, later coding them to your re-search questions. Verify these decisions with a colleague, a prin-cipal, or even students.

The goals for this part of the inquiry process are to:

1. ensure that you are not missing important data nor are you trying to code too much data,

2. gather enough evidence for final analysis, and

3. engage and involve others (students included) in the ac-tion research process in order to validate the importance of teacher research in your school and the community at large.

Conversation Starters . . .

- If you have begun to collect descriptive (anecdotal) data, share samples with a partner and help each other begin to color code the data to the research questions. If you are collecting quantitative data (like Lori's and Audra's), decide on a coding process that you think will compare and contrast your data.

- As a group, discuss who you think might most benefit from having at least a small responsibility in verifying some of your data coding. You might also discuss how you will present this request to your principal.

- Talk about your ambivalence in sharing your data and your projects. What is the worst that can happen? What is the best? How do you ensure that this process is successful?

Chapter 6

Analysis of Findings: Leaving Nothing Undone

"Good Bear learnt his Twice Times One—
But Bad Bear left all his buttons undone".

(A. A. Milne, 1924)

Step 9.   Reread all the sections coded to each one of the questions. Now, look for patterns in the responses you have coded to the questions and decide on categories or themes that emerge within the patterns. Categories or themes help you to summarize and conceptualize patterns of learner response.

Analysis of data is neither mysterious nor difficult; in fact, as a teacher, you do it all the time. Looking for patterns is a typical human response to learning. The question is: Are you looking for patterns of response to guide your instruction? And, What categories emerge within the patterns to help you describe what you are seeing? At this stage of the research process, it is critical that you consider yourself knowledgeable, open-minded, and in charge.

There are no right and wrong answers here, but it is important that you try to leave all preconceived ideas behind while you work through this simple analysis task. What lies in front of you is the most valuable information you have thus far about your research problem or situation, and you don't want to overlook anything due to previous conceptions or assumptions about student learning, behaviors, or your own teaching. One teacher explains the utility of color coding and data organization: "By using the color-coding system, I was able to track patterns right away from the material I was gathering. This really is a tool teachers use all the time, but in our heads."

Charting the Data

At this stage in the action research process, your data will more directly address your questions and you can build simple data charts, like Stacy's in Figure 6.1, or Karen's in Figure 6.2, to develop organizational categories.

Figure 6.1. Data organizer.

Research Question 1: How does the use of Powerful Writing (Treat, 2001) influence the organization of student writing?

Data Source	Teacher Summary of Coded Findings
Anecdotal Records (teaching journal)	There's an obvious gain in the students' technique in writing in a more organized fashion. The program did an excellent job in demonstrating the use of topic sentences and summaries.
Student Assessments	Students were able to assess themselves effectively. They recognized their individual growth in story organization. Sample: On one self-assessment a student wrote, "I need to add a conclusion to my paragraph."
Growth in Writing Traits Rubric (see chapter 5)	The rubric I used to capture the growth in the writing traits of the Powerful Writing program showed a great deal of growth in organization. Powerful Writing charts and examples on topics helped a great deal.

Karen's research questions about the use of miscue, retelling, and reader/teacher responses to miscues are represented by the categories of:
1. oral reading responses,
2. comprehension responses,
3. teacher responses, and
4. teacher decision-making ideas.

By charting the data in this way, Karen is better able to organize and focus what would have been a great deal of information from the RMA conversations held with Nathan. She is also able to clearly see patterns of learner response emerging over time and explain them within specific categories.

Figure 6.2. Charting reader response to expository text: RMA session 3.

Oral Reading Patterns	Comprehension Patterns	Karen's Responses to Reader During Discussion of Text	Information for Instructional Decisions
Reverts to weaker graphophonic strategies in oral reading when there is no context for meaning. Lots of reversals. Looks for little words in big words.	N. explained that he didn't understand the story from the beginning, and so he pronounced words because they looked like others he knew, or he recognized word "chunks."	No picture clues with this reading, which was confusing for N., as he pointed out in RMA session. Do repetitions signal he is trying to make sense or that he is developing a new strategy— checking or rereading the word to confirm meaning?	Prior knowledge and/or picture cues essential for developing context in struggling readers. Without these, ordinarily strong language processes (syntax and semantics) break down. Chunking words seems to be a more logical, meaningful graphophonic strategy for N. rather than stretching words or sounding out.
Placeholders are usually graphophonically similar in beginning letters/sounds to the text word.	Word "whales" read inaccurately was discovered after prior knowledge of the subject was introduced. N. explained his earlier reading: "I was trying to think of the word; I looked for words I know, but I didn't know much about whales then."	Lack of picture clues seemed to confuse him during first read. For unfamiliar text, he is again "chunking," but there just wasn't enough context to help him	Prior knowledge and/or picture cues essential for developing context in struggling readers. Without these, ordinarily strong language processes (syntax and semantics) break down. No cold reads without prior knowledge or pictures. Need to scaffold for vocabulary support. Even chunking doesn't "work" if there's no context. Good time to discuss that reading is "getting meaning."

In looking again at the data from her first inquiry, Karen found that naturally recurring patterns in each of the oral reading and discussion sessions emerged. For example, over time, Nathan's use of placeholders was strongly evident. Another was his tendency to read contractions as two words.

Another example of verification through learner response patterns was demonstrated in Kelli's research inquiry (chapter 4), in which anecdotal records and student writing responses (her two data sources) consistently documented Brandon's performance in two different instructional settings. For example, if you are studying one child's interaction in a small group versus individualized instruction, simply list what happens during each setting, look for patterns, and categorize your findings. This represents a simple synthesis of data, identification of patterns of learner response, and categories that help you label what you're seeing. As teachers, we do this "in our heads" all the time, but actually taking a little extra time to chart the responses and look for patterns—if only in that one student who puzzles us—opens up all kinds of "aha" moments and instructional ideas.

This categorization process works for analysis of findings in a variety of classroom research settings. For example, if you are studying comprehension, then chart examples of learner response under each one by group, or by child, depending on your purpose. What comprehension patterns emerge? Marilee found increasingly complex questioning abilities of the children emerging. She could categorize this pattern under the types of questions the children asked by examining examples of their questions.

If this seems too complicated and time-consuming, please don't stop reading. Instead, compare the process to this metaphorical scenario: You are at a dinner party and know very few people. Don't you start listening for patterns of conversation and categories or topics that you might feel confident in discussing? Do you try to learn more about the participants so you are better equipped to engage in the conversation of the next dinner party? The analysis and synthesis process is really second nature to human behavior.

More on Viewing Patterns and Creating Categories or Themes

If you have collected scores on specific assignments or tests, then you might set up your findings for comparison/contrast as Audra and Lori did. Their research questions were:

1. What effect does cross-age tutoring have on the reading motivation of second graders?, and

2, What effect does cross-age tutoring have on the reading comprehension skills of second graders?

Their existing roster of student scores and dates made it simple for them to calculate ratios of improvement, sustaining, or declining for each area under comprehension (i.e., attitude, context, fact, inference, conclusion, and sequence). They then figured percentages for each area to determine how many students had sustained, improved, or declined in scores. Patterns of strengths and weaknesses emerged, as did categories for organizing their data. They found:

1. that comprehension percentages in general rose from 56% to 74% for the second-grade class when reported as aggregate (combined) numbers, and

2. while attitudes toward recreational reading and buddy reading also improved substantially, attitudes toward academic reading were not as high as Audra and Lori had hoped, but they had sustained.

Using this simple analysis, they could pinpoint the weakest and strongest areas of comprehension for the group as well as for individuals, within the two categories of comprehension and attitude.

When we view student learning outcomes as evidence of effective instruction, patterns of learning become clearly visible. In the next scenario, Laura explores the influence of vocabulary strategies on student learning during literature circles.

Meet Laura

Laura, a third-grade teacher, described the data patterns she found in an action research inquiry focused on how to support vocabulary development during literature circles. She asked the students to use specific vocabulary development strategies as a part of their literature conversation time. As a result of her project, not only did the students' confidence and vocabulary grow, but Laura realized the value of creating study guides and organizers for the children to practice what they were learning during literature circles. Laura explains her experience in looking for data patterns:

The most important pattern I noticed was the confidence children had in the words they had generated. When we began the vocabulary study, some of the children did not put forth the effort I was hoping for. They had to redo the dictionary activity that I planned for each session. When we did the self evaluation, the two children who redid the chart both stated that the dictionary activity helped them understand words in the story. I named this pattern "confidence" which turned out to be one of the strongest themes of my study. My anecdotal notes on story discussions led me to the conclusion that the children needed a study guide to review at home. I noticed some of the children using these study guides during class time to review the words.

Laura also developed a response sheet to chart and categorize her own responses to the data patterns. In addition, a peer reviewer sheet is provided for constructive remarks and observations. These are included in Appendix A.

Triangulation of Data

Findings will be more meaningful if you view the data in multiple ways, particularly as you prepare to share it with other teachers or parents. For example, in Karen's first inquiry, Nathan invariably used placeholders as a word-solving strategy in every oral reading session. This also emerged in his oral reading miscue analyses and later in his discussion about the text, in which he explained his rationale for words he substituted. It is important to be complete in exploring your findings; that is, look for recurring patterns in, and across, the various data sources to verify your findings.

The formal term for this process is "triangulation" of data. Triangulation may be accomplished in a variety of ways. Using three or more data sources, look for verification of findings in each source. The following example comes from Christy's action research inquiry into linking phonemic awareness to greater success in reading and writing at the primary level.

Remember Christy?

You were briefly introduced to Christy, a kindergarten teacher, in chapter 4. Christy triangulated her data using four data sources, which, incidentally, were instructional tools she was using prior to the inquiry. The data sources included:

1. a letter/sound assessment,

2. a phonemic awareness assessment,

3. a reading and writing rubric scale, and

4. her anecdotal records. She remarked that many times her findings from one source were verified by another, but prior to her classroom research inquiry she had never triangulated student learning outcomes by comparing information across these sources. She has since adopted this practice as a typical part of her instruction and assessment routine.

Step 10. Discuss your identified patterns with a colleague to see if you have overlooked something or misinterpreted your data. It is helpful to engage the assistance of someone with whom you have previously discussed your inquiry and sample data coding. *Always* protect the anonymity of the students when discussing scores or other personal data.

As we saw from the conversation between Stacy and Connie in the preceding chapter, it is important to view your data through the perspectives of others early in the project. Then, at the end of your inquiry, when you have charted your data and identified patterns and responses, if possible, ask the same colleague(s) to verify the patterns. If there are discrepancies between what you have identified and what your data reviewer suggests, find someone else to take a look at specific sections and offer their opinion. Colleagues who act as data reviewers keep us honest. These conversations also encourage other teachers to conduct classroom research when they see how empowering and enlightening it can be.

Who Can I Ask to Review the Data?

I previously suggested asking a trusted colleague to review samples of your coding or forming support teams of teachers who meet as study groups to share their coding, findings, and the research process in general. While the support teams are generally the most helpful, there are other people who may serve as excellent "reviewers," particularly if you are the only person conducting classroom research in your building. These include knowledgeable parents, principals, curriculum coordinators, university professors, or student teachers who would benefit not only from your research but also from your professional example.

Teachers who conduct reciprocal information sharing show themselves to be professionals in the highest sense of the word. They are proud of what they do, particularly in their role of change agents. Far too often, teachers are viewed as complacent curriculum technicians instead of researchers involved in making sound instructional decisions daily—decisions that ultimately affect our communities, our culture, and our lives.

Chapter Summary

If your findings are to be reliable, you must code the data and analyze them for patterns. To verify your coding and analysis, ask a colleague, a principal, or a teacher from another school to review your findings. This will help you see patterns of response that you missed, or raise questions that need to be answered before you can make instructional decisions based on your data analysis. Form study groups in your school or district to serve as peer reviewers and a support system for classroom research.

Conversation Starters . . .

- If you have started a classroom research inquiry, find a colleague who is also conducting classroom research and discuss how you will code your data. If you have begun the process, ask your colleague to comment on your coding.

- View some samples of student work that address a curriculum objective. Look for patterns of learning that are verified across these potential data sources.

- Brainstorm how a classroom research study group might be formed in a school. Develop some initial steps to follow in forming a study group.

Chapter 7

Implications to My Teaching and Learning: What Nuggets of Gold do I Behold?

Classroom research is a democratic process in that it illuminates the voices of many learners and allows the teacher to listen and look at learning responses through multiple lenses (Arhar, Holly, & Kasten, 2001; Watson, Burke, & Harste, 1989). Teachers are only human: We tend to take a stance that is familiar and comfortable. As a result, curriculum is typically designed around specific objectives, and learning outcomes measure responses to the teaching of those objectives. In reality, there is much more happening in that classroom.

"Good research, like good curriculum, invites participants to speak" (Watson, Burke, & Harste, 1989, p. 35), and when they do, we can examine their language, their voices, and their learning as we explicate our own ideas and beliefs about the relationship between teaching and learning. Sometimes, simply by virtue of examining our beliefs through our actions and the responses of children, we formulate a whole new set of understandings and a whole new base of knowledge as we rethink and carefully examine our classrooms through our own inquiries and research (1989).

Step 11. Look at the data responses, and again, note the patterns you have identified and the categories that help organize the learner responses. Now, beneath each one, list their implications to you for teaching and learning.

Start by looking at your patterns of responses and the names you gave them. To see implications, turn the kaleidoscope wheel and compare learner response patterns to lessons or instruction occurring at the time of response. What were you doing and what happened as a result? Then look for successful learner response patterns. What kinds of curriculum and setting seem to "work" best for each child? Remember Kelli (chapter 4), who thought that Brandon needed lots of one-on-one instruction, only to find that his comprehension and interaction was much higher in small group settings? This was an implication to her teaching and provided many clues to structuring curriculum practices to better benefit Brandon. These are implications that guide instruction.

What nuggets of gold do I behold? Useful classroom research is revealing. It gives us direction as teachers and learners and invites us to mine the finest ore of our teaching beliefs.

Remember Cindy?

Cindy was interested in whether or not comprehension could be explicitly taught to first graders using specific strategies. These included think alouds, using post-it notes for prediction, "say anything," which helped students brainstorm details, and story pyramids for story grammar. Through a simple action research project, she learned that comprehension was something that *could* be taught using these strategies but *not* until students—not their teacher—had established a clear purpose for reading. In other words, she believed in the theory behind the strategies, but prior to her inquiry she had not understood her role in the process. Key to making the strategies work for the students was *their* understanding that when they made concrete, real-life connections to the text, they established a purpose for reading.

Cindy's classroom inquiry had an immediate effect on her teaching. She began to ask prereading questions that prompted these connections, such as when introducing a book about time of day, she asked, "What is your favorite time of day?", instead of her usual, "What do you think the book is about?" This led to increased comprehension, ownership, and independence in reading for her first graders. The patterns in her students' comprehension development clearly showed an increase when personal connections and purpose were established prior to reading.

Back to Marilee

If you recall, to develop her classroom inquiry, Marilee kept anecdotal records on the children's responses and behaviors and, for baseline data, she assessed their comprehension at the beginning and end of the three-month inquiry with an informal reading inventory. At the end of three months, most of the children's comprehension had increased by one or two reading levels, and their cognitive responses to narrative text were progressively more sophisticated during reciprocal teaching. They learned to ask a variety of questions—both literal and inferential and to respond thoughtfully to one another. While these results might be applicable only to this group of children, it was enough for Marilee to use Reciprocal Teaching (Palincsar & Brown, 1984) and Direct Explanation (Duffy, Roehler, & Herrmann, 1988) wherever she could in her daily teaching because of the confidence and gains it gave this particular group of struggling readers.

Classroom research provides us with information about our teaching that we may assume or overlook. One of the teachers dubbed these oversights as "teaching miscues."

Viewing Our Own "Teaching Miscues:" Karen

Karen coined the term "teaching miscues" during her second classroom research inquiry. So many times, what she thought she was doing as a teacher was not evidenced in data gathered from student responses during Retrospective Miscue Analysis (RMA) sessions. For example, she wanted to be able to help students understand that reading was making sense of language. She thought she was continually doing this by demonstrating various reading strategies and talking about how well the children used the strategies to gain meaning. However, when she asked them what reading meant to them at the end of the research inquiry, they said it was "sounding out the words and finding big words in little words." Dumbfounded, she listened to taped recordings of herself working with students and discovered that this strategy was indeed the one upon which she relied most heavily. This chapter will discuss how to go beyond our research findings and discover the implications they hold for us as teachers.

How Does Classroom Research Keep Us Honest?

I would like to address that question with a classroom research story of my own. I developed a classroom research project one semester early in my career as a teacher educator. In the study, I examined my teaching actions through the written perceptions of preservice teachers, then compared them with my own research journal responses. During the first two months,

my journal entries were full of examples describing my interpretations of their comments through my eyes and my preconceived
ideas. For example, the students frequently asked to "participate
in more activities." A characteristic research journal response of
mine was, "I'm not sure what students mean by more activities. I
believe that I always have the students practice strategies we're
learning, but I am trying to get them to think of their own ideas
and potential teaching situations." When I began to analyze the
data by comparing their responses to mine, I was chagrined! Their
responses were rich resources for how I could improve the learning in our classroom, and I had, for almost two months, virtually
ignored them. I vowed to do two things:

1. code the data as I went along, and

2. change my instructional plans!

Calkins (1983) says that "awareness of one's own thinking
marks a crucial step toward directing it" (p. 136). From this classroom research experience, I became acutely aware of the tendency to focus on the act of teaching rather than on the beliefs
behind it. Actions are easily defined, sorted, and modified and
beliefs are not. Finding, then examining, the intuition that drives
the action presents a unique challenge that begins with carrying
out a classroom inquiry and extends to include some process for
examining the beliefs behind the actions.

Chapter Summary

This chapter focuses on how we look at our findings as teachers and ask what they mean to us as teachers and learners. What
changes do they suggest or what kinds of teaching actions do
they affirm? As teachers and researchers we continually look for
patterns of learner response. A familiar pattern is "the right answer," but sometimes children give us unexpected answers. What
patterns are evident in these answers? What interesting information does this provide us about children and learning?

Conversation Starters . . .

- Whether you are a veteran teacher or a novice, you have undoubtedly discovered the reality of "teaching miscues." Think about a time when you, or someone else, had a "teaching miscue" moment. What happened?

- Videotape your own teaching for a day. What kinds of patterns emerge that you were unaware of?

- Calkins (1983) says that "awareness of one's own thinking marks a crucial step toward directing it" (p. 136). What questions do you have about your own thinking about teaching?

Chapter 8

Going Public

"Teachers spend day after day in complex isolated worlds of meaning making that for the most part go unrecognized for their wealth of insight and knowledge about the learning process."

(Hubbard & Power, 1999, p. 177)

Step 12. Share classroom research information with peers and colleagues in a setting that honors the importance of the research process as well as the findings. Keep your principal informed and involved as well.

Clearly telling the story of what you learned will keep this wealth of insight and knowledge from being easily dismissed. As previously discussed, sometimes small groups of teachers meet as study groups to share their information. Sometimes teachers shared their findings during faculty development presentations at state or national conferences. Just keep in mind that names, personal information, and scores should be reported anonymously.

Peer Support for Classroom Action Research

Action research provides us with a means and method for conducting classroom research that lends itself to being shared informally because it is a part of classroom instruction and assessment. Just as we exchange teaching tips and ideas, what you learned by studying a particular strategy or setting can be disseminated in the same professional manner. Sometimes 10 or 15 minutes of time during regular faculty meetings are sufficient with follow-up conversations and questions via E-mail, during recess duty, or as a visit to the researcher's classroom. The important thing is sharing what is learned from your classroom research with the purpose of improving learning and teaching while giving others ideas to begin or to further research in their classrooms.

Small group meetings are excellent vehicles for shared discussion, but it is important that names, personal information, and scores be reported anonymously, unless formal permission from parents, participants, and the school has been secured. It is also integral to honor and value each person's contribution to the discussion. Questions, ideas, and conversation thrive in this kind of learning scenario.

forming Teacher Researcher Study Groups

A group of nine teachers from two neighboring schools decided to meet twice a month after school to share and support their classroom research procedures and findings. They invited me to participate. Their projects were first attempts at action research and ranged from examining strategies for teaching algebra in fifth grade to strategies for managing the disruptive behaviors of a single student. Not always were their stories happy, but this group provided a safe haven to vent frustration and to ask for help.

They discussed how they were individually "customizing" the methods and tools of action research to meet their needs and schedules, the kinds of patterns they were observing in learner response, and how they were changing their teaching, parental contact, or ways of interacting with students as a result of their findings. These two schools were also part of a combined effort between two neighboring districts to post their action research projects on a common Web site in an effort to share their information with other professionals, parents, and the community at large.

Comments from teachers substantiate the value of meeting to share research findings and hurdles. Steve, a sixth-grade teacher, explains:

> *These meetings are powerful. We talk about what each one is doing but also we validate each other and offer suggestions, either for the research part or for teaching. We take away a ton of useful information and we learn how to be*

more reflective. I was really out of sorts with my project during the first three weeks. I didn't think my data sources and questions were going anywhere. This group helped me rework my questions, and the data sources lined right up to fit!

Glynis was introduced in chapter 3. She conducted a classroom action research project on teaching algebraic concepts through reciprocal teaching and manipulatives (Appendix C). She adds her comments to the discussion about going public:

Sharing information with colleagues and principals also makes us feel like true professionals. Our colleagues value what we are discovering and help us with our questions. I've had other teachers ask me about my classroom research on helping fifth graders acquire algebraic skills. At first, they just wanted to know what I found out, but when I show them how I discovered a simple research process for monitoring the teaching of this difficult concept, they are all ears.

Greg, who you also met in chapter 3, used the study group meetings as a peer-review process for his classroom research. He describes the benefits of the meetings:

During this meeting time, many staff members gave me suggestions about my research questions and aided me in determining ways of triangulating my data sources. Each of these teachers thought my project was strong and even picked up some ideas of their own.

Affecting the Teaching and Learning Culture

Sharing information from action research projects often gives other teachers the impetus for taking risks and trying new ideas or strategies. No matter how interesting and informative the workshop training you received might be, implementing a new program is not always a seamless process. However, when a trusted colleague offers assurances that learning responses will be positive and that they are willing to discuss their experiences and research outcomes, then risk-taking is not so daunting. Action research has the power of changing and guiding the school culture in subtle and empowering ways.

In the vignettes which follow, Trayce and Lisa provide examples of the influence of classroom research on school culture, while Karen's research marked the beginning for change in one student's instructional interventions.

Meet Trayce

Trayce was the only first-grade teacher in her building willing to try out a new writing program. The program had been adopted by the intermediate-grade teachers, but the primary teachers were not convinced it was developmentally appropriate. Trayce conducted an action research project during the implementation process and learned that this was indeed a sound instructional procedure. Her enthusiasm in sharing the positive findings from her inquiry led other first-grade teachers to implement the program in their classrooms. She comments:

> *I have already discussed this entire topic with two other first-grade teachers that I work with. I have shared lots of examples of my students' work with them, and I have shown them the improvement that was made in such a short time. They, too, are looking forward to implementing this writing program in their classrooms next year!*

Meet Lisa

Lisa, a K–8 reading specialist, sought to find ways of including teachers' observations and assessments in the evaluation and referral process for Title I reading services in a large inner city district where she taught. She was frustrated because some of the children who needed services the most were not placed in a resource classroom, due to the district's reliance on a single standardized test score for placement. With the help of other teachers and her administrator, Lisa compared results from teachers' informal assessments on struggling readers who did not make the Title I "cut" based on standardized test results. The findings from her inquiry raised the awareness of parents, administrators, and teachers of the need to diversify the assessment process and to trust the teachers' judgment of student development as much as they did standardized test results.

Remember Karen?

Karen's first inquiry into Retrospective Miscue Analysis (Goodman & Marek, 1996) showed that empowering a reader to discuss miscues regularly and with others greatly impacted the motivation and achievement of a struggling reader. Prior to Karen's work, this reader was one step away from a self-contained special education classroom. Today he is enrolled in a "regular" classroom with sustained, proven intervention measures resulting from Karen's inquiry. When findings from the data analysis in Karen's, Trayce's, and Lisa's classroom inquiries were shared with other teachers and decision makers, positive educational change resulted.

Keep Your Principal Informed and Involved

Sharing the classroom research process with your principal helps create a space for action research in your school and validates his or her role as an educational leader. Consider asking the principal or curriculum coordinator to serve as a peer reviewer at various stages of your data gathering and analysis and even as your final reviewer. You may be pleasantly surprised at how much they learn about, and comment upon, your knowledge and expertise as a teacher. Engaging administrators in classroom research offers rich opportunities for talking about teaching and learning within the context of your action research inquiry, rather than within the less meaningful context of a standard teaching evaluation form.

There were five principals and one elementary curriculum coordinator involved in the professional development school model, *Teaching and Learning Communities,* in which many of the teachers you have met in this book conducted their action research inquiry. Each one of the administrators was supportive and respectfully inquisitive about the project outcomes, and they all became involved in the data analysis and sharing process at some level. One read all of the projects, provided feedback on data coding and analysis, and helped make arrangements to post the projects on a shared Web site. He well understood the relevance of teachers studying their own learning to the growth and development of children.

Other principals attended the graduate course in action research taken by some of the teachers to better understand the projects and to support their development. Two became regular members of the research study group meetings in their buildings. For all but one of these principals, action research in the classroom was a new and unfamiliar concept, but, as strong instructional leaders, they were interested in learning more. When teachers cautiously began to share pieces of information from their research inquiries, and later, invited principals to take a look at the data, the support system for classroom research grew strong in these schools.

Not all administrators are knowledgeable about the process or the value of classroom research; however, when they are given information that links student success to teacher research, interest is sparked. Most principals are reluctant to add more to the teachers' workload, so classroom research must be explored as a way to create stronger professional development opportunities for teachers utilizing existing classroom routines and resources. Take Karen's situation, for example. She was the only teacher in her building out of 40 who was quietly conducting classroom research. Her principal knew she was doing some sort of reading research, but until she gained state and local attention by presenting her results at conferences, he was noncommittal. After she presented the findings of her second inquiry at an international conference and was accepted for publication in a major journal, she became, in his eyes and those of other teachers, an example of what it means to be a teacher researcher and the added value that classroom research brings to a school community. Karen's colleagues began inquiring about her work with Nathan and, later, asked the local university about providing a short course in classroom research using Karen's research as an introduction.

Raising Awareness and Support for Classroom Research

The key to raising awareness for the need to offer teachers time and support for conducting classroom research is to provide hard evidence of the effect it has on student learning, professional development, and the community of the school. Enlist the aid of a teacher or a team of teachers who have conducted classroom research. Many professional development schools have integrated action research into their mentor virigule teacher training. Most likely, they, as well as their principals, will be willing to share research experiences and offer helpful advice for beginners. For example, the teachers from *Teaching and Learning Communities* spoke to other schools and teachers about their success and satisfaction with this process. They also shared their initial uncertainty about their ability to conduct classroom research. Ultimately, they reassured principals and teachers that once you take a focused look at your teaching by utilizing action research methods, you never think of your teaching, or of student learning, in the same way. As the teachers pointed out, it costs no more than a day or two of in-service training and the reassurance that their efforts and shared information will be honored, valued, and supported.

"Show what you know" is my best advice to those who will be breaking new ground in their school communities. Be able to demonstrate how classroom research will benefit your school because of what you know of the process, or by what you are already doing and would like to do better. Most people like to see visual representations from the results of action research projects like those shown in this book and to talk to real teachers who are classroom researchers.

Validating Classroom Research

Action research quickly became a socially and educationally validated part of the schools who were a part of the professional development school, *Teaching and Learning Communities*. This was largely attributed to the fact that principals talked with one another about the action research projects going on in their school, then compared the learning and research outcomes across other schools. The curriculum director and principals actively sought ways of further sharing information within and across districts. For example, one teacher was asked to share her findings with all K–2 teachers for a districtwide in-service day. The teachers in this same district planned and presented another half day of in-service training to others in their district as well as preservice teachers, during which time several teachers presented the beginnings of their action research inquiry findings and how they set up their inquiry. For those teachers participating in *Teaching and Learning Communities*, a Web site was authored by school resource staff and supported by central administration for posting the action research projects. Other teachers, like Karen and Vicki, have presented their classroom research findings at major state, national, and international teacher education conferences and, because they are "real teachers," they were well received by colleagues and university faculty alike.

Teachers and principals may ask how they might share their classroom research findings with parents and other community members. There are actually three ways that work. The first method is traditional: Invite parents to read about your research in a newsletter or make it a part of parent-teacher conferences. You might create a special presentation for Open House in which several teachers post or share the kinds of research projects they are conducting. (This may also be created as an on-line resource.) The second method is also fairly standard—sharing information at Individual Educational Plan (IEP) meetings, or school and community situations like Lisa's, in which student achievement scores determine their access to resource services.

While the first two methods work reasonably well, they do not actually involve the parents in the research process. The third method challenges teachers to take a risk and develop a different way of thinking about research participants. For example, four elementary classrooms situated in three different schools actively involved family or community members as informal research participants. Drawing from the work of Wollman-Bonilla (2000), as well as that of Shockley, Michalove, & Allen (1995), family members exchanged message journal entries with kindergarten and first-grade students as a part of four classroom research projects.

To begin the project, the teachers sent a letter home introducing and describing the Family Message Journal project (Wollman-Bonilla, 2000) to parents, asking them if they were interested in participating. With only a few exceptions, the results were overwhelming. Parents, siblings, cousins, grandparents, aunts, and uncles wrote to the children, making connections between their lives, what they knew about school, drawing elaborate illustrations, and adding information to the topics the children were studying. The teachers shared the success of the Family Message Journals with the families via regular notes home, letting them know that this was a new project and that they were a part of the process of discovery and change. Some teachers mentioned the term "classroom research," but others simply involved parents in this authentic literacy event as an instructional method. Janeen built another action research inquiry around Family Message Journals. Her complete project is found in Appendix D.

Parents learned firsthand about their children's literacy development, while also being shown how teachers conduct informal classroom research to enrich children's learning. They became a part of the classroom; therefore, they were a part of the classroom research process. Parents and other family members also learned about their children's school, their knowledge, and the importance of family connections between teachers, students, and school. In the rare occasions when family members did not write, the school counselor, the custodian, the principal, and the school secretary acted as back-up writers. No child was without a response to read and learn from.

The same teachers are eager to continue the projects, possibly engaging community members, such as university students or business professionals, who are willing to be a part of their research into authentic literacy contexts to support emergent language and writing.

Chapter Summary

Action research always yields important information within the context of classroom research and learning. In this chapter, teachers as change agents view their research as important data to be shared with others in settings which value and honor the professionalism of teaching and learning. Whether or not the results of all classroom action research may be directly applied to other students and classes is not our issue. Most important is the understanding that we learn a great deal from one another when we go public with our research procedures and findings. Ideas are born and questions are asked.

Teachers are in the unique position to effect change that might not have otherwise occurred. As you are developing a system for documenting and studying patterns in daily teaching and student learning, others may learn to implement similar processes. This cycle holds powerful potential for impacting student learning and the integrity of teacher knowledge. All it takes is a commitment to sharing what we are learning about ourselves and our students.

Conversation Starters . . .

- Is there a policy or program in your school that could benefit from the scrutiny of an action research inquiry like Lisa's? Think of something that involves more than one teacher and how you might work together, as Lisa did, in acting as change agents.

- Discuss or think about how you can actively involve the community in classroom research projects. Family Message Journals is only one of many ways. What about family history projects, shared book experiences, or book clubs managed by volunteers such as family or community members?

- Enjoy Janeen's classroom research inquiry on Family Message Journals in Appendix D, and discuss the various ways parents become involved and possibly enlightened by their involvement in the research process.

- Advocacy is a hot topic in teacher education today. How can sharing your classroom research with members of the community, as well as members of your profession, achieve greater understanding of, and advocacy for, authentic teaching and learning?

Chapter 9

Embracing the Role
of Teacher as Researcher

"What a long time whoever lives here is answering
this door." And he knocked again.
"But Pooh," said Piglet, "it's your own house!"
"Oh!" said Pooh. "So it is," he said. "Well, let's go in."

(A. A. Milne, 1926)

Teachers who conduct classroom research have accepted the invitation to claim their classroom spaces in an effort to better know themselves as teachers and to learn from their students. The teacher researchers from whom I have drawn research examples for this book all said they never viewed teaching in the same way after conducting action research in their own classrooms. Following are some examples:

Karen

Karen thoughtfully described this perspective on classroom research through the term "teaching miscues." She noted how, through classroom research, she discovered the many times she misinterpreted her own actions. "Until I started taping and reviewing reading lessons, I did not realize how much I *led* the reader. I was doing all the talking!" For Karen, teaching and researching are synonymous with learning about who she is as a professional. Now, as a well-respected teacher researcher in her district and state, she often shares her action research projects at national and international conferences as well as with teach-ers from her district and school.

Janeen

Like Karen, Janeen has conducted several classroom action research inquires. Her most recent focused on how to motivate second-semester kindergarten children to write by making daily, written connections with family members. (Her project is included as Appendix D.) Here's how the inquiry came about:

After attending a local in-service workshop in which Cindy presented her classroom research about making home and school connections, Janeen wondered if her 13 kindergarten children could engage in a similar process. Cindy had discussed her re-cent action research project in which she had developed and stud-ied the use of family message journals (Wollman-Bonilla, 2000) with first-grade students. After a few conversations with Cindy, Janeen launched her inquiry utilizing her reflective journal, the children's letters, and letters from home as data sources. The children wrote daily messages to a family member, such as a parent, a sibling, a grandmother, a cousin, or in one case, a pet! The designated family member responded to the message regu-larly, having previously agreed to participate faithfully. Figure 9.1 is representative of the quality and care that went into the messages, both from the children and from family members.

Through this inquiry project and others, Janeen confirmed her beliefs that authentic reading and writing with a purpose is the most developmentally appropriate way to teach literacy. By including community members as research participants, Janeen validated and broadened the research outcomes with an unex-pected bonus—family and community connections. Parents and other family members commented on how they enjoyed this strat-egy with detailed, positive comments on what they were learn-ing about the language and writing potential of their child. Family members were also discovering more about their kindergarten member and their relationship with that child through their mutual writings. Janeen reports that some parents told her that conversations from the message journals extended into family mealtimes and other events.

Figure 9.1. A child and parent's responses to the family message journal.

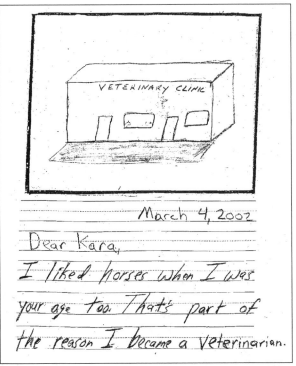

March 4, 2002

Dear Kara,

I liked horses when I was your age too. That's part of the reason I became a veterinarian.

Dear Daddy,
Thank you for the horse.
Love,
Kara

March 1 2002
DEAR DADDY
THNK U FOUR
THE HrS
LOVE KArA

Remember Lisa?

Embracing the role of teacher researcher involves believing in your interpretation of findings and the importance of those findings to teaching and learning. Lisa (chapter 8) provides us with an exemplary model of risk-taking, decision making, advocacy, and professionalism. Lisa was one of the first middle school teachers I worked with in designing an action research inquiry. She knew from the onset that her inquiry would involve and impact a number of people, but from our first meeting she insisted that "teachers' observations and understanding about student learning must be heard." Her role was one of advocate, and others appreciated the professional framework for exploring teacher knowledge that her research inquiry provided.

As a result of Lisa's inquiry into the need for multiple forms of assessment for placement in reading resource classrooms, new assessment guidelines for evaluating children's eligibility for participation in Title I programs were implemented in her district. The results of her inquiry were later chosen as evidence to support a major grant proposal for her school district. This provides an excellent example of the power that teachers, as knowledgeable decision makers, wield. Lisa's evidence of how teachers were much more accurate and reliable predictors of children's need for remedial reading assistance than a single set of standardized test scores is but one example of how "going public" with our research gives credence to our profession and defines our role as classroom researchers.

A great deal of the classroom research process entails building relationships of trust between teachers, students, school, and community. It is apparent that Karen's, Janeen's, Cindy's, and Lisa's schools are well on their way to embracing the role of teacher as researcher as a part of their culture. And, for these teachers, classroom research has become an integral, and natural, part of their teaching lives.

Chapter Summary

Our classrooms belong to us and to the learners. Through action research, the identity of these precious "spaces" is clarified and strengthened. In particular, our actions as teachers are defined and studied in a safe, protected manner that can only lead to better instruction. Unlike standardized assessment results, we are finding information directly related to the curriculum we teach. By now, you must have a much clearer understanding of how the process of action research affects professionals as a whole, while supporting strong and democratic classrooms that extend into the community and beyond.

Conversation Starters . . .

- When have you been frustrated with standardized test results that represented the child as a score, rather than detailing his or her learning? Where do you see classroom research making a difference in this scenario?

- Invite your principal to join a classroom research study group meeting or, during a meeting, brainstorm ways to engage the principal in the process, thus gaining greater support for your efforts.

- Why is it important to embrace the role of classroom researcher? How does embracing the role of classroom researcher establish your identity as a professional "change agent" with integrity and knowledge to share? What do you see as challenges to this role?

Chapter 10

Further Questions: One Good Inquiry Leads to Another

Action research inquiries formally end with results and implications, but classroom research and its outcomes carry potential for raising all sorts of new questions. Those questions lead classroom teachers into the realm of continual professional development within the readily available laboratory of the classroom and the school. This chapter will examine questions which emerged as a result of various classroom studies, summarizing how three studies were built upon them.

By now, Janeen, Karen, and Cindy's classroom research projects are familiar to you. Upon closer examination, you may notice that, over time, their classroom research inquiries might easily be characterized as individual professional development plans. Studying our own teaching is one of the most powerful forms of engendering positive change in schools. It is a ready resource that claims few resources and those that it does, like time, training, shared information, and reflection, are returned many times over.

Janeen studied the teaching of writing through inquiry with young children for several years within the context of writing workshop, journal writing, environmental print, and creative labeling, as well as other strategies. With the help of Connie, a fifth-grade teacher and colleague, she was ready to move forward with new questions about the effects of multiage grouping within an outdoor setting on the literacy development of her students, as well as a group of fifth graders.

Next, drawing from her experience with multiage grouping in writing, she extended her questions about the development of language and literacy in young children to include an inquiry into family message journals. "One good inquiry certainly leads to another," Janeen remarked with a smile.

Karen, who is currently completing her third consecutive inquiry into Retrospective Miscue Analysis (RMA), continually refines the research process as she seeks ways to reach struggling readers. Each year, she selects new questions to pursue about the features and instructional potential of RMA. She has a well-defined role as reading resource teacher, informally utilizing her research data as a springboard into conversations with classroom teachers who are wondering how to reach the struggling readers in their classrooms. It is Karen's hope that these teachers will realize kernels of understanding that will help them to better understand the reading process. In Karen's first inquiry, the child who puzzled her the most read choppily with surprisingly good comprehension. Karen learned that the reading perceptions of this student changed when he was given the opportunity to discuss his miscues and retellings with her. This inquiry led to the second, which focused on what a small, mixed-ability group of children would discuss when reviewing their various miscues and how that influenced their understanding of the process of reading and writing.

Currently, Karen is studying the use of RMA with cooperative learning groups whose members choose most of their own miscues for discussion and interpretation. In addition, she asks the students to revisit their retellings for different or greater interpretations of the readings. She has held on to one question throughout each of these studies: How do RMA conversations influence and guide student response to the *process* of reading and writing? Karen continues to investigate how the children perceive reading and how those perceptions influence their reading responses and choices. She says that findings from all three studies have led her to helping children take greater risks in talking about their reading, increasing their collective vocabulary through group discussion of miscues, and in widening their reading interests to a greater variety of genres. She continues to advocate for the importance of reader response in the acquisition and development of language and literacy, sharing her questions and data with classroom teachers, administrators, and curriculum directors, thus providing them with informal and formal assistance in the teaching of reading in the large inner city school in which she works. She, like many of the teachers introduced in this book, also serves as a resource person to the local university.

Cindy continues to use the analysis of running records as both an assessment and teaching tool, but as I mentioned in the last chapter, recently became interested in building stronger home and school connections. Cindy's classroom is representative of a continuous plan of classroom research and professional development.

Often teacher inquiry is sort of a "rebirth" process in which questions from one inquiry directly build on another. How you build those connections is influenced a great deal by your interests, your students, and your teaching situation in general. It is up to you to make the kind of meaningful connections between research topics and your teaching. For example, Cindy explained that the analytical and reflective process of reviewing running records had led her to question the influence of family culture and language on developmental patterns in children's oral language and reading. As a result, she designed a classroom inquiry to monitor the use of family message journals in her first-grade classroom. These journals became "text" for reading and springboards into writing about home, school, and community. Parents, peers, and teachers came together in the literacy learning process to share letters, ideas, information, and voice. Vocabulary, spelling, and writing developed naturally and authentically as children read their letters in small groups and brainstormed ideas for new letters.

Cindy has since extended her classroom inquiry questions to explore frameworks for teaching comprehension strategies to first graders. From her classroom inquiry into home and school connections have come creative ways of sharing the responsibility of literacy learning with parents. Cindy developed excellent communication with parents as a result of the family message journals project because they were important, involved players. Now, as part of her current classroom research, she is investigating ways to involve parents in supporting the new strategies for comprehending expository and narrative text. For Cindy, the process of inquiry and information sharing is ongoing as one inquiry leads to another.

In summary, all the teachers with whom you have become acquainted in this text say that classroom research helped them become better teachers, and for most, the tools and processes of action research have become a way of teaching and knowing. It's like Barbara, a veteran kindergarten teacher, explained in chapter 2: "We do all these things almost daily as teachers, but I just never knew how to organize what I was observing in such a way that it systematically informed my teaching."

Chapter Summary

This chapter deals with the idea that we build on research as a normal part of teaching and learning. Classroom research vitalizes teaching and learning as one inquiry always leads to another. Teachers who implement action research with success begin to look on the process as a part of their teaching lives. It is a fluid, natural process which always leads to new questions, answers, and further inquiry.

Conversation Starters . . .

- What further questions do you have about classroom research?

- If you have been reading this book while conducting action research, form small study groups and list what you have learned about yourselves as teachers.

Appendix A

Reproducible Charts
for Data Collection
and Organization

I.   Observation Chart for Identifying Data Sources

II. Various Data Organizers:

- Anecdotal Record Summary

- Written Response T-Chart for Research Partners

- Data Chart for Recording Research Questions, Topics, and Pattern Analysis

- Questions, Data Sources, and Summary Charts

- Reflective Response to New Vocabulary Strategy Implementation With Peer Reviewer Response Sheet

Organizer for Identifying
Classroom Data Sources

Date   **Learning Event**   **Research Question Addressed**

_____

_____

_____

_____

_____

_____

_____

_____

_____

_____

_____

_____

_____

_____

_____

_____

_____

_____

_____

_____

_____

_____

_____

Anecdotal Record Summary

Date	Learning Event	Teacher's Action	Student Response	Teacher Response	Evaluation of Interaction

Reflective Written Response
T-Chart for Research Partners

Name of respondent:

Date:

Advantages Impacting Teachers and Students

(The topics listed are examples. Please provide your
own comparison topic.)

Topic: Basal Instruction	Topic: Inquiry- and Literature-Based Instruction

Disadvantages/Advantages for Teachers and Students

Basal Instruction	Inquiry- and Literature-Based Instruction

Data and Findings Organizer

Research Question:

Data Source	Teacher Summary of Coded Findings

Alternative Question, Data Source, and Summary Chart

Research Question	Data Sources Used	Summary of Coded Findings

Data Chart for Comparing Research Question Topics and Viewing for Pattern Analysis of Teacher or Student Response

Research Question: _____

Topic	Topic	Teacher Responses	Information for Instructional Decisions

Note: The two patterns that Karen studied were oral reading and comprehension. You might wish to study other comparison topics such as: understanding of math process and accuracy of response. This chart is designed to help you see patterns and clearly contrast them in two different contexts.

Reflective Response to New Vocabulary Strategy Implementation With Peer

Reviewer Response Sheet (by Laura Sadler)

Strategies currently in use:

_____

_____

_____

New Strategies Implemented	Date	Reflection on Results of Strategy Implementation

Peer Reviewer Response Sheet

Strategy Implemented	Date	Peer Reviewer's Response to Researcher's Observation

Appendix B

(Sample Classroom Action Research Project)

Inquiry- and Literature-Based Instruction Versus Basal Instruction in a Fourth-Grade Social Studies Class

By Victoria Seeger, with Jessica Starr (student teacher)

Introduction

We chose to study the use of inquiry- and literature-based instruction versus basal instruction in the social studies content area for three reasons:

1. the recent textbook adoption by the school district was not meeting student needs,

2. integrating content areas through literature-based learning allows more in-depth study to occur and focuses most classroom learning within a day on the topic rather than limiting the topic to 45 minutes a day, and

3. the scope of the information in the basal is limited.

Background Information

"Content is not an end. Content is a vehicle for further inquiry." (Costa, 1999)

We used two Web sites to find background information on inquiry- and literature-based learning. The first Web site details information that supports the use of inquiry-based learning, including a definition and how it differs from traditional classroom learning.

The two Web sites are: "http://www.thirteen.org/edonline/" and "http://books.nap.edu/". These sites provided us with clear definitions of the two learning methodologies so that we were better able to focus our own reflective responses to the disadvantages and advantages of both.

The contrast between learning from a textbook and inquiry-based learning is great. It is essential to note that learning from a textbook is often appropriate and necessary; however, the benefits of inquiry-based learning are many. The problem with textbook learning, as we see it, is the focus it takes and where it stops. Students are often asked to learn facts, dates, and background information, but then the student is not asked to apply or analyze that information. Learning facts often does not require students to interpret the data or draw conclusions (or, the text offers both *for* the students). Vicki writes, "As I reflect upon how I have used textbooks in our classroom, I now understand that part of the problem is that I have halted the learning because of the *way* in which I have used the basal."

Inquiry-based learning naturally involves students in finding out what is important to them, allowing students to guide the learning. Finding out is only part of the process, however. Students need to be taught to go beyond the data-gathering phase and convert what they have gathered into knowledge learned. In turn, "Educators must understand that schools need to go beyond data and information accumulation and move toward the generation of useful and applicable knowledge . . . a process supported by inquiry learning" (http://www.thirteen.org/edonline/concept2class/month6/index.html).

Add to the inquiry-based model the use of literature (outside of the basal), and students have powerful sources to begin the process of understanding what they have learned. It is interesting to note the differences in ways in which students respond to authentic literature sources as opposed to information found in a basal. During a recent reading lesson using *Jumanji* (Van Allsburg, 1981), students were genuinely disappointed to find out that their copy of the reading material was in their basal literature book (even though it contained the entire text). They referred to the teacher's copy of the actual book as a "real" book.

During a recent native Kansas animal research project, students were incredibly motivated to seek out information from "real" books and Internet text sources for their research. The learning "buzz," while often frenetic, was so inspiring to watch. We cannot compare it to textbook learning on the same topics, but the students became researchers; knowledge and facts were not imparted *to* them. Students were empowered to learn and analyze text for the information they needed.

The resources Vicki has read on inquiry-based learning and the frustrations she has observed and experienced while teaching with a textbook lead her to the conclusion that inquiry- and literature-based learning is a method that needs to be implemented in our classroom in a concerted way. We hoped to see an increase in student involvement and interest as well as more in-depth learning taking place.

Setting

The setting for our classroom inquiry was in a fourth-grade open classroom in a suburban school district with 1,763 students. The elementary school has 300 students in a K–6 setting; there are 44 students in the classroom. The school has a very low occurrence of students at-risk because of socioeconomic status. In fact, most students are from middle- to upper-middle class homes. There were 44 students in the classroom (24 males and 20 females), two classroom teachers, and a student teacher from a local university.

Research Questions and Data Sources

We developed the following research questions and data sources after discussing what was already available and what we might want to add as evidence of student learning and attitude in the two types of instruction, inquiry and basal methods. The data charts used for the study are included at the end of this project. They are a student survey, a T-Chart for our responses, and our anecdotal record-keeping form.

Research Question 1: What are fourth graders' perceptions of the advantages and disadvantages of using inquiry- and literature-based learning in Social Studies?

Data sources:

- Student questionnaire
- Anecdotal notes kept by teacher and student teacher during inquiry- and literature-based learning (see Appendix A for sample notes)
- Student products from inquiry- and literature-based learning as well as copies of worksheets and assessments from basal instruction, including student scores from those assignments

---

Research Question 2: What are the advantages and disadvantages of an inquiry- and literature-based unit versus basal instruction from a teacher and student-teacher point of view?

Data sources:

- Written responses using a T-diagram model (see Appendix A for an example). This represents two sources; one is Jessica's response column and one is Vicki's.

Research Question 3: How are readers impacted by an inquiry- and literature-based unit versus basal instruction?

Data sources:

- Results of Fry Readability Graph from Social Studies basal samples
- Results of Flesh Reading Ease and Flesh-Kincaid Grade Level scores from Social Studies basal samples
- Progress Report data (in reading and Social Studies) (see Appendix A)

Period of Time for Data Collection and Baseline Data

The data collection for the inquiry- and literature-based unit occurred from the beginning of a study of the southwest region of the United States, March 25, through April 19, 2002. Basal instruction (in the Social Studies content area) had occurred from the beginning of the academic year up to the point the southwest region study occurred. Samples of worksheets and assessments, and scores from these, were taken from previous units as baseline data.

Data Gathering and Analysis

Data for the project were color coded according to their relevance to the research question. Data for Question #1 were coded in blue; data for Question #2 were coded in pink; and data for Question #3 were coded in orange.

There were two peer reviewers for this action research project: our principal and a teaching colleague from another school.

We began collecting data in the form of anecdotal notes on the day the unit began. We found that we were duplicating some notes, so we took turns recording data. If we heard a specific comment or observed some behavior pertinent to the study, we recorded it, no matter who was "officially" recording that day.

The anecdotal records we kept of student comments and responses during the unit showed the high level of student interest in the inquiry process. Students were very engaged in this unit, and their comments indicated the amount of research they were doing outside of the classroom. The anecdotal records were, however, a bit difficult to code. We thought they would serve as a useful tool to find out information about the basal versus inquiry instruction, but their primary purpose ended up as a record of the students' enthusiasm for the unit.

Changes We Made Along the Way

We changed one data source during the project because as we began recording, Vicki realized that it "fit" under two questions. Portions of the student questionnaire actually answered two questions. The rubric portion applied to Question #1, while the written portion was useful for Questions #1 and #3. We also moved the data sources having to do with readability to Question #3. While the basic readability impacts how a teacher perceives instruction, it carries more weight in influencing how a reader perceives the basal.

We coded the data using the three colors of highlighters indicated. Even though we thought the data collection devices would each apply to only one question, we were actually able to code for all three questions from the data organizers.

Results/Findings

The results of our project are summarized under each of the research questions which follow. Within each summary, we have designated patterns which we found consistent to the data.

Research Question 1: What are fourth graders' perceptions of the advantages and disadvantages of using inquiry- and literature-based learning in Social Studies?

The questionnaire given to students produced data overwhelmingly in favor of inquiry- and literature-based instruction versus basal instruction; however, half of the students said that they liked the tests and worksheets associated with the basal. Only three students disagreed with the statement "I like the activities and projects that we use when we study literature and use inquiry in Social Studies." The results of the rubric portion of the questionnaire in which students were to rank their perceptions of the two methods of teaching and learning Social Studies are listed below. They are followed by a summary of the students' written responses to open-ended survey questions. The two kinds of data helped us qualify and quantify their responses as well as triangulate the data.

Student Survey Question #1: "I like it when we use our Social Studies textbook to study the United States regions."
Strongly Agree = 4
Agree = 11
Neutral = 2
Disagree = 21
Strongly Disagree = 6

Survey Question #2: "I like to study the United States using literature and inquiry."
Strongly Agree = 24
Agree = 16
Disagree = 4

Survey Question #3: "I like the worksheets and tests that we use when we study with the Social Studies textbook."
Strongly Agree = 6
Agree = 18
Disagree = 16
Strongly Disagree = 4

> **Survey Question #4: "I like the activities and projects that we use when we study using literature and inquiry in Social Studies."**
> **Strongly Agree = 32**
> **Agree = 9**
> **Disagree = 2**
> **Strongly Disagree = 1**

Patterns did develop in the students' written responses on the questionnaire—some students stated that they liked the text because it was new and updated (this basal was newly adopted). What the students stated they liked about the literature, inquiry, activities, and projects also showed patterns. They clearly liked the projects, specifically the brochures and flip books. Another frequent response was getting to use the Internet to conduct research. A few poignant student responses caught our attention.

"You wind up reading a good book [we held book talks on Dust Bowl literature]."

"When I use a resource, it helps me know what it means. Helping me think more . . . It really helps when we use resources."

"It helps me understand."

"It hooks you in."

Five students mentioned liking the group work, and one student noted that they were able to get up and move around. Other common themes in the responses were: the students had fun; they liked the opportunity to be creative; they enjoyed the artwork.

Research Question 2: What are the advantages and disadvantages of an inquiry- and literature-based unit versus basal instruction from a teacher and student-teacher point of view?

We both answered questions on a T-diagram about the advantages and disadvantages of the two types of instruction in Social Studies. The advantage of using basal instruction is in having a "package" to teach from, including worksheets, overhead transparencies, and assessment sources. Preparation time was noted by both of us to be the main advantage to using the basal. Students all have access to the same materials when using basal instruction (i.e., text, pictures, maps, graphs, etc.).

The disadvantages of using basal instruction are that the information presented is basic, lacks depth, and does not cover a significant range of topics. The textbook is written above grade level and is difficult for many students to follow and understand. Another disadvantage is that there is little opportunity to pursue or acknowledge students' interests. A good teacher will pick up on this during basal instruction, but if there is no opportunity for discussion, the life/world connections will be overlooked.

The primary disadvantage of an inquiry- and literature-based unit is the amount of time a teacher will spend researching and creating the unit. The creation of this kind of unit requires accessing information from a variety of resources. The other disadvantage noted by both of us is the time involved in assessing the projects created with this kind of a unit. Rubrics must be created, written feedback given, and assessment is more subjective because you are not scoring worksheets. Other disadvantages listed were trying to help a student get caught up following an absence, and it is possible that a topic will be overlooked.

The advantages of a unit driven by inquiry and literature center primarily on the involvement of students in the process of inquiry. Students are engaged in the process because they "own" the topics being researched and seek out information from resources they choose. Another important advantage is the connections students make between what they are studying and their own world. They brought in many items from home, information from parents, grandparents, aunts, and uncles, and information they sought out on their own from the Internet, the public library, and books from home. Students also made strong connections between the literature read to them and their projects. They would often ask to borrow a book to get a drawing just right. The amount of cooperative learning required of students was greater during a unit using inquiry. The learning taking place seemed more productive, as the talk among students within the classroom was on-task time rather than off-task.

Research Question 3: How are readers impacted by an inquiry- and literature-based unit versus basal instruction?

We did not expect to glean so much information from the student questionnaire about the textbook itself. While the readability of the basal information is significant, what students had to say about their textbook is fascinating. Patterns developed in the students' written responses on the questionnaire. The things they listed most often that they liked about the textbook were the pictures and maps. Students mentioned that they could "look up" information in the text. Students also picked up on the assistance the text can give them, mentioning the highlighted words, "the answers are always there," bold lettering, words to learn (vocabulary), definitions, and captions. One student stated, " . . . It is a quick tool to use."

The readability information we learned from various data sources mentioned earlier is perhaps the most significant evidence to emerge from this project. The current Social Studies basal is not written for fourth-grade students.

Readability of the Basal

The overall readability and reading ease ratings were conducted on three passages in the Social Studies textbook being used by the fourth-grade class in the identified school district. This is a new textbook adopted for the 2001–2002 school year. Tools used to determine readability level were the Fry Readability Graph (Fry, 1989), Flesh Reading Ease (McCarten, 2000) score, and Flesh-Kincaid Grade Level (2000) score. Representative sample results are listed below.

The *first sample* was taken from page 68 in the textbook:
Fry Readability Graph results: Grade 17+
Flesh Reading Ease score: 62.9
Flesh-Kincaid Grade Level: 7.1

The *second sample* was taken from page 237 in the textbook:
Fry Readability Graph results: Grade 16
Flesh Reading Ease score: 66.5
Flesh-Kincaid Grade Level: 7.1

The *third sample* was taken from page 397 in the textbook (it is important to note that this sample is from a piece of literature that is embedded into the textbook):
Fry Readability Graph results: Grade 6
Flesh Reading Ease score: 78.2
Flesh-Kincaid Grade Level: 5.4

Note of Explanation: The Flesh Reading Ease score guidelines indicate that the higher the score on a scale from 1–100, the easier the text is to understand. For standard texts to be understood, the aim is for a rating of approximately 60–70.

The data patterns indicate that the textbook being used is not appropriate for fourth-grade students. While using the textbook this year, Vicki noticed that students struggled to read the text in whole-class instruction and often needed prompts to pronounce words within the text. Most of the class is reading at grade level, but the results of the readability tests clearly indicate that the textbook is written beyond the fourth-grade level. While it is widely stated that textbooks are written two grade levels beyond the grade they are intended for, this textbook's readability test scores suggest that it is written well beyond two grade levels. It was impossible to allow any independent reading of the text and understandable that students were also having difficulty with worksheets and assessments that were a part of the series, as they are written in a similar fashion as the text. After teaching a unit, Vicki commented that she and a partner teacher (who team taught with her) were often frustrated with student assessment scores. They knew that the material had been taught, but students were not doing well on any kind of daily worksheets or assessments given. Vicki said that they were often left in a position of altering their expectations to make students feel successful with the material.

Implications to Teaching and Learning

We have affirmed what we believe from this action research project: Basal instruction is only minimally effective in engaging students' interest and attention, and the basal is not grade-level appropriate reading for them. From the moment we began the Mysteries of the Southwest unit, we knew students were engaged in the learning process, having fun, and being creative in the process. It was so easy to connect this unit to all of the other content areas and activities that we do in our classroom, that we could feel the success the students were experiencing from the beginning. Authentic learning is driven by what students want to know and not imparted by the teacher to the students. We learned as much throughout this unit as the students.

The idea of creating theme units based on each region of the United States was something Vicki has wanted to do for a long time. She explains:

I worried about assessment and how students would re-spond. This unit and the action research project leave me with no doubt about how I will proceed with teaching So-cial Studies next year. It is clear that students like the text-book as a "tool," and it will become a resource for them, but I will be using inquiry and literature to teach Social Studies in the future.

The information on the readability of the text is probably the most important implication to others in the field. The informa-tion may change how another teacher uses the text or the worksheets and assessments that are integral parts of it. We would hope that teachers could see the bigger picture, though, and at least try inquiry one time during the year. It is time-con-suming, however, and may not appeal to all teachers' sense of instruction and assessment.

further Questions: Vicki

I would like to keep data on assessment during the inquiry- and literature-based units that I do. I also want to keep track of how I teach reading and language arts during the Social Studies units to see how and when integration is occurring. I will need to be careful to cover all of the mapping skills that fourth graders are expected to know on standardized tests. Also, I may use MAT7 (Metropolitan Achievement Test) assessment data regularly gen-erated by our district to examine how students achieve in the area of Social Studies from third grade to fourth grade.

Student Questionnaire for Action Research: Mysteries of the Southwest

Date: _____

Directions: Please answer the questions below to help us evaluate our Social Studies learning.

A. Indicate if you agree or disagree with the statement.

I like it when we use our Social Studies textbook to study the United States regions.

|————————1————————2————————3————————4————————
Strongly Agree   Agree   Disagree   Strongly Disagree

I like to study the United States using literature and inquiry.
|————————1————————2————————3————————4————————
Strongly Agree   Agree   Disagree   Strongly Disagree

I like the worksheets and tests that we use when we study with the Social Studies textbook.
|————————1————————2————————3————————4————————
Strongly Agree   Agree   Disagree   Strongly Disagree

I like the activities and projects that we use when we study using literature and inquiry in Social Studies.
|————————1————————2————————3————————4————————
Strongly Agree   Agree   Disagree   Strongly Disagree

B. Please respond to the following two questions. Write thoughtful answers please.

• The things I like best about our Social Studies textbook are (list 3 things):

• The things I like best about using literature, inquiry, activities, and projects to study Social Studies are (list 3 things):

Mysteries of the Southwest: Anecdotal Records Form for Action Research Project

Record sheet used by: Vicki Seeger, fourth-grade teacher and Jessica Starr, student teaching intern. (This form is a variation of one found in Appendix A.)

Date	Activity or Project	Student Response	Student Comments	Teacher Observations

References

Costa, A. L. (1999). How people learn: Brain, mind, experience, and school. *Commission on Behavioral and Social Sciences and Education.* (http://books.nap.edu)

_____http://www.thirteen.org/edonline/concept2class/month6/index.html

Fry, E. (1989). Reading formulas—maligned but valid. *Journal of Reading, 32,* 292–297.

McCarten, E. (2000). Reading assessment options. (http:zzchd.gse.gum.edu)

Van Allsburg, C. (1981). *Jumanji.* NY: Houghton Mifflin.

Appendix C

(Sample Classroom Action Research Project)

Teaching Algebra in Fifth Grade:
Reciprocal Teaching and Manipulatives
By Glynis Kickhaefer

Introduction

I chose to research this topic, because to demonstrate skill in using algebraic concepts is one of our state-mandated goals for Grade 5. I recently participated in a workshop called *Making Algebra Child's Play* (Borenson, 1999; Montney, 2000) to help me teach some of these concepts. This is a hands-on approach to teaching algebra to elementary students. I was excited about the opportunity to provide students with greater choice and decision making in an area in which they were not yet confident. This method of teaching algebraic concepts empowers students to take charge of their learning, thus placing the teacher in the role of facilitator after basic skills are introduced.

Background Information

To increase my facility with this approach, I read two articles recommended by the workshop facilitator. These are listed in the References.

Setting and Participants

The participants were a class of 21 fifth graders assigned to small groups of 8 to 10 students.

Baseline Data

I gave the students a teacher-made algebra preassessment. Out of 21 students, 20 failed the test, completing only between 0–2 problems correctly. The one child who scored 6 out of 10 had some exposure to algebra in fourth grade at another school. The students were also given a survey to record their attitude toward "algebra" before lessons were taught and after they had exposure to the *Making Algebra Child's Play* (2000) lessons.

Resources

- A math kit developed from workshop information and instruction

- Materials I developed along with another teacher who was also implementing the program

- Teacher-made (Kickhaefer) pre and post assessment of knowledge

- Teacher-made (Kickhaefer) pre and post perceptions survey

Procedures and Data Analysis

I gave the students a prealgebra test recording their scores on a chart. Then, I taught four lessons given in the *Making Algebra Child's Play* workshop kit (2000) during the next six weeks. We spent approximately an hour on each of the lessons. Initially, I introduced the lessons in manipulatives and instructed the children in the use of reciprocal teaching, in which they were taught to take over the modeling of different problems through various questioning techniques—utilizing the hands-on approach. Reciprocal teaching involves students taking turns as "teachers" and asking questions of their peers. This process generated many grand conversations as they worked, questioned, argued, and problem solved together. Of course, I would mediate when needed to keep them on-task. At the end of the study, I gave the students a posttest as well, asking them to fill out my teacher-made perceptions toward algebra survey. The survey asked the students to examine how much they thought they knew about algebra before and after they began the lessons in reciprocal teaching and manipulatives.

The spring semester was an ideal time to conduct this project, because I was fortunate to have a student teacher. While I was working with a small group, she was working with the rest of the class. We would switch groups the next day, thus giving us each more one-on-one time with our students.

My data analysis was simple: I compared results from the pre and post assessments of: 1) ability to perform algebraic tasks, and 2) the students' attitudes toward algebra.

Findings/Results

From my baseline data, I found that most children had heard the term "algebra" before, and knew that letters were used with numbers, but that was the extent of their "pre" knowledge. Twenty out of 21 fifth-grade students did not understand algebraic concepts at the beginning of the lessons in March. At the end of four lessons, or about six weeks, 19 students passed the beginning algebra test with flying colors. The 2 students who did not understood the processes of algebra, but their inability to master basic facts kept them from getting correct answers.

In addition, their perceptions of what they knew about algebra changed dramatically. At the beginning of the study, not one student felt they had a good understanding of algebra. By the end of the study, 15 students reported they were confident enough in their knowledge to teach algebra to others.

Self-Perception Survey Results: N=21

Before: 4 students said they knew nothing about algebra.
After: 0 students said they knew nothing.
Before: 7 students said they had heard the term algebra but did not know what it was.
After: 0 students said they had heard the term but did not know what it meant.
Before: 10 students said that they knew a little bit about algebra—they knew letters were involved.
After: 2 students said they knew a little bit about algebra—they knew letters were involved.
Before: 0 students said that they had a really good idea and could do most of the problems correctly.
Before: 0 students said they could teach algebraic concepts to others.
After: 15 students said they could teach algebra concepts to others.

Implications

Using this hands-on method allows the teacher to see exactly where a student is "getting stuck" and helps that student get back on the right track. Utilizing reciprocal teaching empowers students to take charge. When they were encouraged to use manipulatives to problem solve as they practiced reciprocal teaching, they quickly began to use more accurate algebraic vocabulary and demonstrated to other students how to problem solve. This made the student a more powerful learner. After using this program, the fifth graders were confident in their knowledge of algebra skills and demonstrated that they knew the material well enough to teach it to others.

References

Borenson, H. (1987, May/June). The gifted child today. *EDPRESS*, *10*(3), 54–56.

Borenson, H. (1999). *The hands-on equations learning system*. Borenson and Associates, P140, Penndel, PA, 19047.

Montney, E. *Making Algebra Child's Play*. Conference held in Topeka, KS, Fall 2000.

Appendix D

(Sample Classroom Action Research Project)

**The Influence of Family Message Journals
on the Reading and Writing of Second-Semester
Kindergarten Children**
By Janeen Horton

Introduction

Just as the flowers were beginning to bloom last spring, I observed a similar occurrence with the blooming of beginning readers and writers in my kindergarten classroom. Throughout the school year, we have had multiple opportunities to explore the concept of transferring the spoken word into written form; but, in the same way that the buds on those flowers need spring showers and sunshine to prosper, my students were in need of a sprinkle of excitement to continue their writing growth.

The previous fall, I had attended a workshop led by Cindy Pounds, a first-grade teacher in my district. Cindy spoke of an approach to offering authentic reading and writing opportunities called Family Message Journals (Wollman-Bonilla, 2000). She shared many of her students' journals as examples. As I flipped through the pages, I saw in-depth conversations between students and their family members. Cindy explained how the process worked, piquing my interest. Could this approach be slightly adjusted and adapted for use in kindergarten?

I asked Cindy if I could borrow her book, *Family Message Journals—Teaching Writing through Family Involvement* (Wollman-Bonilla, 2000). After reading more about family message journals, I began to figure out ways to make this approach appropriate for kindergarten students. The possibilities for literacy development seemed limitless. I decided to try it, framing an action research inquiry around the process to keep me honest and knowledgeable about the results.

Participants and Setting

The participants in this study were 13 students in the morning session of kindergarten and 15 students in the afternoon session in a rural elementary school in the Midwest. Elmont Elementary serves approximately 200 students who are generally white, middle class. The kindergarten consisted of 17 girls and 11 boys. At the beginning of the study, as determined by placement on a developmental writing scale adopted and used by our district, all 28 students were within the precommunicative stage of writing. More specifically, 6 students were at the beginning level (i.e., requiring frequent assistance, needing encouragement, demonstrating beginning understanding), while 22 students were more at the developing level (i.e., requiring some guidance, willing to try, understanding concepts and skills). Additionally, I used a stages-of-reading scale used by our district in placing 3 students at the pre-emergent reading stage and 25 at the emergent stage. One of the pre-emergent readers was at the developing level, while the other 2 were at the secure level (i.e., understanding, applying, and extending concepts and skills, demonstrating independent work habits, self-motivated). All 25 emergent readers were at the beginning level.

Other participants included the families of these students. Of the 28 students, 23 live with both parents. The remaining 5 have single parents or live in a joint-custody situation. Many of the children wrote to siblings, aunts, uncles, cousins, and even pets! A great many people actually participated in this study.

Research Questions

Research Focus: Family Message Journals

Research Questions:

1. How does the implementation of family message journals affect kindergarten students' writing progress?

2. How does the implementation of family message journals affect kindergarten students' reading progress?

3. How does family involvement in ongoing authentic reading and writing opportunities affect kindergarten students' enthusiasm toward reading and writing?

Data Sources, time frame, and analysis

Data Sources:

1. My written observations and anecdotal records while evaluating a reading of a passage from the journal on the district progress report reading scale

2. Sample writings (evaluated on the district progress report writing scale)

3. Parent/student conversations

4. My teaching journal

Time frame for the inquiry:

February 25, 2002 through April 18, 2002 (six instructional weeks)

Baseline Data: I compared pre and post baseline data on the District Kindergarten Progress Report.

Data Analysis:

I reviewed my anecdotal records weekly to identify and code patterns and connections of observations to the research questions. I coded by placing the number of the research question to which I was referring in the margin of my reflective journal and observation notes. I met with a colleague (peer reviewer) weekly to reflect and confirm the data patterns. At the completion of the study, I compared initial writing samples with final samples to determine what changes had occurred. In addition, I compared pre and post baseline data on the District Kindergarten Progress Report. I contacted parents via E-mail, telephone, and face-to-face conversations for additional input. As I analyzed the data, three themes emerged:

1. writing growth,

2. reading growth, and

3. family involvement.

Findings/Results

I. Writing Growth

I looked first at how the implementation of family message journals affected kindergarten students' writing progress. Taking my precommunicative writers into this process was, to say the least, a challenge. I needed to "dangle a carrot" in front of these writers to get them to think in terms of writing complete thoughts. Family message journals gave them this incentive.

Additionally, I needed to prepare them for working in small groups (usually five to six students) during Literacy Center times and providing adequate support to each other.

The first couple of sessions, we concentrated on letter writing form (i.e., date, greeting, body, closing). These first sessions were somewhat hectic. Most of the students chose to write some form of "I love . . ." as a message, feeling safe with this statement. My reflections in my teaching journal, anecdotal records, and observations guided me to streamline my minilessons to give my writers a nudge in utilizing independent writing strategies to take risks with their writing—like looking back at previous messages to spell words, using "Star Word" cards, stretching out words, and helping each other. Most of my observations were of students putting into practice what we had practiced all year—using consistent letter/sound relationship to "guess and go" for temporary, invented spelling.

At the end of the six weeks, I rated the students' writing once again to determine writing growth. One student had jumped to the secure level of the next stage, semiphonetic. The most exciting news was that the 27 remaining students had leaped up two stages, to the phonetic stage! Broken down further, 8 writers were at the beginning level, 12 at the developing level, and 7 were at the secure level.

II. Reading Growth

Next, I examined family message journals' effects on reading progress. At the beginning of each session, I would assist each student individually in rereading their previous message and the family member's response. Very often, the "Star Words" were circled, so I knew that the child had already read the message at home. Many times, I noted that students would go back after writing and reread all the messages. All of the children would track the print from left to right and top to bottom. The authentic passages had so much meaning for them that using context was easier. Also, words and names with personal importance to each individual student were in many entries, so the readers were able to practice them repeatedly.

I asked each kindergartner to read the last entry to me to rate on the reading scale. The 3 pre-emergent readers had moved up to beginning emergent readers, while the other 25 previously beginning emergent readers improved to the developing level. I was most pleased with the fact that so many of the students were consistently able to recognize frequently used sight words. I have never had such success in this area.

III. Investment in Reading and Writing by Children and Families

The final area to consider was how family involvement in ongoing authentic reading and writing opportunities affect kindergarten students' enthusiasm toward reading and writing. Before the students took the journals home for the first time, I sent an informative letter to prepare them. Another letter was attached to the front of the journal the first time it was taken home. (These are included at the end of this writing.) Because the parents were so willing to participate in this process, as was evidenced by the consistent participation, the family enthusiasm was contagious.

This approach gave parents a way to be involved in ongoing reading and writing development without the struggle associated with helping children with traditional homework. The modeling and joint project of writing back and forth made for *purposeful* writing. The children wanted to continue conversations with family members because there was a focused audience just for that writing. Enthusiasm was also increased, since the topics pertained to individual interests and needs. Students enjoyed asking questions, telling jokes, and thanking others for giving or doing something. The bottom line on enthusiasm was that the students were excited to work in their Family Message Journals in the Literacy Center time rotation.

Implications

The implementation of Family Message Journals has fit right in with the teaching beliefs I have been developing over the last couple of years. More specifically, I believe that the use of meaningful, purposeful, authentic reading and writing is the most effective way to teach young children. By putting into practice developmentally appropriate programs and strategies, like Family Message Journals, the students are inspired to relate verbal conversations to the written word.

So now what? I am not sure that we would have the success that we experienced if I tried to begin writing in the journals earlier in the year. The prior opportunities to explore with picture writing and labeling those pictures enabled the students to advance to the point where parents, overall, would be able to recognize the child's writing as somewhat conventional. The background knowledge was a key factor in the success. Therefore, I plan to send Family Message Journals home in the spring semester, just as I did this year.

By using Family Message Journals, I have been able to adjust my teaching to incorporate appropriate minilessons to meet student needs. The students internalized so much more (i.e., sight words, letter/sound relationship, conventions of print, understanding that print holds meaning) because they were applying it to a meaningful situation. The addition of Family Message Journals to my language arts program has been a success!

References

Wollman-Bonilla, J. (2000). *Family message journals: Teaching writing through family involvement.* Urbana, IL: National Council of Teachers of English.

Parent Letters

February 25, 2002

Dear Family,

This is my family message journal. I will be bringing it home once a week. Ask me to tell you about my message and drawing. Please print a short note back to me, and draw a picture along with it, if you'd like. Read your note with me a few times to reinforce my reading skills. I will reread your message to Mrs. Horton when I bring it back to school. It is requested that you PRINT your message, and use a letter format by including the date, a greeting, the body of the letter, a closing, and a signature.

Mrs. Horton also told us that our journals live in our backpacks. They will come out for a visit at home, and go to bed in my backpack at night. This way, I am sure to have my journal each time I am ready to continue my letters to you! Could you please help remind me to pack up my journal whenever I bring it home? Thanks for being a part of my reading and writing!

Sincerely,

February 25, 2002

Dear Family,

I have come across an exciting approach to teaching reading and writing through family involvement. I recently read a book called *Family Message Journals* by Julie Wollman-Bonilla. The idea presented in this book is that young writers need ongoing opportunities to experiment with print, trying to match sounds to letters, and to express their ideas in writing legibly and clearly for themselves and for others. Family Message Journals provide these opportunities for writing by providing a real audience for that writing.

Here's how it works: At school, your child will write a message to you. Then, we will send the journal home, and you will write a message back. Once a week during Literacy Center time, I will work with small groups to write a message to each child's family. Keep in mind that I am encouraging the students to become independent writers by using the sounds that they know to print their message. This "invented (temporary) spelling" helps them make letter/sound connections and understand that writing is just a way to get your thoughts down on paper. As your child works through his/her writing, I will have him/her read the message to me, and I will print it in "conventional spelling" on a sticky note so that you will be able to read it. Next, your child will bring the journal home and read it to/with you.

Your job will be to respond on the next page to your child's message. I will attach a note to let you know when we will need your message returned to school. Most likely, we will need your message one week from when your child brings the journal home. Your message is not being evaluated—only appreciated! Don't worry about your spelling, grammar, or punctuation. It is the content of your message that will benefit your child. Remember to respond to their topic. For example, if your child's message is about hibernation, and you write back about having pizza for dinner, then your child isn't getting a chance to communicate with you through writing. They may think you aren't taking their writing seriously by not responding to what their message was actually about.

Your response may be one or more of the following types of responses:
1. Demonstrate interest—(zzzzz Abby, No, I didn't realize bears hibernate so long. Thanks for the information.)

cont.

2. Provide new information—(Dear Abby, Did you know that the bears at the zoo are hibernating now?)
3. Share personal opinions and stories—(Grrrr Abby, Once when I was little, I read a book about a bear that hibernated too long.)
4. Ask questions and/or offer solutions—(Dear Abby, Do other animals hibernate? Or, Wow, Abby! I think you could find out more about bears at the school library.)

Remember to use the following format that includes the following: date, greeting, body of the letter, closing, and your signature. Here's the example:

February 25, 2002   (date)

Dear Abby,   (greeting)

I learned something new from you today. I didn't realize the groundhog and woodchuck are two dif-ferent names for the same animal!

(body of letter)

Love, (closing)

Mommy (signature)

If for any reason at all you are not able to meet the expectations of a weekly reply, please let me know imme-diately. I will find someone in the school building who will commit and write a message to your child.

I will begin the journals by asking your child to write about what they do at school. Eventually, I will ask them to write a message about various things that they feel are important.

Above all, be creative and have fun with your re-sponses. I am extremely excited about trying this ap-proach. Thank you for helping to assist in your child's reading and writing development. I know that the chil-dren will love to communicate with you in this way.

Sincerely,

Janeen Horton

References

Arhar, J., Holly, M., & Kasten, W. (2001). *Action research for teachers: Traveling the yellow brick road*. Upper Saddle River, NJ: Merrill Prentice Hall.

Bogdan, R., & Biklen, S. (1992). *Qualitative research for education: An introduction to theory and method*. Boston: Allyn & Bacon.

Bourne, B. (Ed.). (2000). *Taking inquiry outdoors*. Portland, ME: Stenhouse.

Brause, R., & Mayher, J. S. (1991). The never-ending cycle of teacher growth. In R. Brause and J. S. Mayher (Eds.), *Search and re-search: What the inquiring teacher needs to know* (pp. 23–115). London: Falmer Press.

Burrow, M. (2001). *The effects of direct explanation and reciprocal teaching on reading comprehension*. Unpublished Masters thesis. June 2001. Washburn University. Topeka, KS.

Calhoun, E. (2002). Action research for school improvement. *Educational Leadership, 59* (6), 18–24.

Calkins, L. (1983). *Lessons from a child: On the teaching and learning of writing*. Portsmouth, NH: Heinemann.

Clay, M. (1993). *An observation survey of early literacy achievement*. Portsmouth, NH: Heinemann.

Clay, M. (2000). *Running records for teachers*. Portsmouth, NH: Heinemann.

Cochran-Smith, M., & Lytle, S. L. (1992). Communities for teacher research: Fringe or forefront? *American Journal of Education, 100* (3), 298–324.

Cochran-Smith, M., & Lytle, S. L. (1993). *Inside / outside: Teacher research and knowledge*. New York: Teachers College Press.

Corey, S. (1952). Curriculum development through action research. *Educational Leadership, 7*, 147–153.

Corey, S. (1953). *Action research to improve school practices*. New York: Teachers College Press.

Darling-Hammond, L. (1997). *The right to learn: A blueprint for creating schools that work*. San Francisco: Jossey-Bass.

Duffy, G., Roehler, L., & Herrmann, B. A. (1988). Modeling mental processes helps poor readers become strategic readers. *The Reading Teacher, 41*, 762–767.

Glanz, J. (1998). *Action research: An educational leader's guide to school improvement*. Norwood, MA: Christopher-Gordon.

Glanz, J. (2003). *Action research: An educational leader's guide to school improvement*. (2nd ed.). Norwood, MA: Christopher-Gordon.Goodman, K. (1996). *On reading*. Portsmouth, NH: Heinemann.

Goodman, Y. (1978). Kid-watching: An alternative to testing. *National Elementary Principal, 57*(4), 41–45.

Goodman, Y. (1996). *Notes from a kidwatcher*. Portsmouth, NH: Heinemann

Goodman, Y., & Marek, A. (1996). *Retrospective miscue analysis: Revaluing readers and reading*. Katonah, NY: Richard C. Owen.

Harp, B. (2000). *The handbook of literacy assessment and evaluation*. Norwood, MA: (2nd ed.) Christopher-Gordon.

Hubbard, R., & Power, B. (1999). *Living the questions: A guide for teacher researchers*. York, ME: Stenhouse.

Lefever-Davis, S. (2002). Trends in teacher certification and literacy. *The Reading Teacher, 56*(2), 196–197.

Lewin, K. (1946). Action research and minority problems. In G. W. Lewin (Ed.), *Resolving social conflicts: Selected papers on group dynamics* (compiled in 1948). New York: Harper & Row.

Martens, P. (1998). Using retrospective miscue analysis to inquire: Learning from Michael. *The Reading Teacher, 52*(2), 176–180.

McFarland, K., & Stansell, J. (1993). Historical perspectives. In L. Patterson, C. Santa, K. Short, & K. Smith (Eds.), *Teachers are researchers: Reflection and action* (pp. 155–159). Newark, DE: International Reading Association.

McKenna, M., & Kear, D. (1990). Measuring attitude toward reading: A new tool for teachers. *The Reading Teacher, 43*, 626–639.

Meyers, E., & Rust, F. (Eds.) (2003). *Taking action with teacher research*. -ortsmouth, NH: Heinemann.

Milne, A. A. (1924). *When we were very young*. New York: E. P. Dutton & Co.

Milne, A. A. (1926). *Winnie-the-Pooh*. New York: E. P. Dutton & Co.

Milne, A. A. (1928). *The house at Pooh corner*. New York: E. P. Dutton & Co.

Moore, R., & Aspegren, C. (2001). Reflective conversations between two learners: Retrospective miscue analysis. *Journal of Adolescent and Adult Literacy, A Journal of the International Reading Association, 44*(6), 492–503.

Moore, R., & Brantingham, K. (2001, May). *Reflective responses to reading miscues*. Paper presented at the meeting of the International Reading Association, New Orleans, LA.

Moore, R., & Brantingham, K. (2003). Nathan: A case study in retrospective miscue analysis. *The Reading Teacher, 56*(5), 466–473.

Moore, R., & Seeger, V. (2003, January). *Teaching and learning communities (TLC): An innovative framework for the preparation and professional development of teachers.* Paper presented to the annual meeting of the American Association of Colleges for Teacher Education, New Orleans, LA.

National Commission on Teaching and America's Future. (1996). *What matters most: Teaching for America's future.* New York: Author.

Palincsar, A., & Brown, A. L. (1984). Reciprocal teaching of comprehension-fostering and comprehension-monitoring activities. *Cognition and Instruction, 1,* 117–175.

Patterson, C., Santa, C. M., Short, K., & Smith, K. (Eds.), *Teachers are researchers: Reflection and action.* Newark, DE: International Reading Association.

Pinnell, G. S., & Fountas, I. (2000). *Word matters.* Portsmouth, NH: Heinemann.

Schon, D. (1983). *The reflective practitioner: How professionals think in action.* New York: Basic Books.

Schon, D. (1987). *Educating the reflective practitioner.* San Francisco: Jossey-Bass.

Shockley, B., Michalove, B., & Allen, J. (1995). *Engaging families: Connecting home and school literacy communities.* Portsmouth, NH: Heinemann.

Shoyer, G., & Yahnke, S. (2001, September). *Professional development schools and student achievement: Do we make a difference?* Paper presented to the annual Kansas Coalition Conference, Olathe, KS.

Treat, M. (2001). *Powerful writing.* Lawrence, KS: Curriculum Solutions.

Watson, D. (1996). Miscue analysis for teachers. In S. Wilde (Ed.), *Making a difference: Selected writings of Dorothy Watson* (pp. 34–55). Portsmouth, NH: Heinemann.

Watson, D. (1996). Reader-selected miscues: Getting more from sustained silent reading. In S. Wilde (Ed.), *Making a difference: Selected writings of Dorothy Watson* (pp. 79–87). Portsmouth, NH: Heinemann.

Watson, D. (1996). Defining and describing whole language. In S. Wilde, (Ed.), *Making a difference: Selected writings of Dorothy Watson,* (pp.183–202). Portsmouth, NH: Heinemann.

Watson, D., Burke, C., & Harste, J. (1989). *Whole language: Inquiring voices.* New York: Scholastic.

Wollman-Bonilla, J. (2000). *Family message journals: Teaching writing through family involvement.* Urbana, IL: National

Council of Teachers of English.

Wyatt, F., Meditz, N., Reeves, M., & Carr, M. (1999). A cohort model for supervision of preservice teachers developed by mentor teachers. *Teaching and Change, 6* (3), 314–328.

Index

About the Author

Rita Moore is an Associate Professor of Education at the University of Montana—Western in Dillon, Montana, where she teaches undergraduate and graduate courses in Reading, Language Arts, and Education. Her research and writing interests focus on teacher research and innovative approaches to teaching reading and writing in elementary, middle school, and high school classrooms. Her own action research is grounded in field classroom settings with teacher colleagues like those introduced in this book. As a public school teacher, Rita taught Reading, Language Arts, and Spanish in the primary and middle school grades as well as high school. Rita and her husband, David, reside in Dillon, Montana, where they enjoy leisurely mountain hikes and wildlife viewing.